SPELLING

DEVELOPMENT, DISABILITY, AND INSTRUCTION

SPELLING

DEVELOPMENT, DISABILITY, AND INSTRUCTION

By Louisa Cook Moats

YORK
PRESS BALTIMORE

The book was manufactured in the United States of America.
Typography by The Type Shoppe, Inc.
Printing and binding by McNaughton & Gunn.
Cover design by Joseph Dieter, Jr.

Library of Congress Cataloging-in-Publication Data

Moats, Louisa Cook.
    Spelling : development, disability, and instruction /
  by Louisa Cook Moats.
      p.   cm.
    Includes bibliographical references (p.) and index.
    ISBN 0-912752-40-8
    1. English language--Orthography and spelling--
    Study and teaching.
  I. Title
  LB1574.M573   1995
  372.6'3--dc20   95-44438
                                    CIP

CONTENTS

Dedication

*Dedicated to Chipper, who after spelling 4 of 20 words correctly
on his 5th grade test, was accused of being irresponsible, lazy, deceptive,
and a true test of character for his teacher;*

*to Chrissy, who failed her riding test because she could not spell
the equine anatomy vocabulary;*

and to Charlotte, whose questions about words deserved better answers.

Acknowledgments

I am grateful to Amy Nichols and Faith Pushee for their help preparing this manuscript; to Erwin Stunkel for his encouragement and generosity in providing me with time to work; to my family for their patience; to Reid Lyon for his personal support and intellectual leadership; to the many teachers and clients who have expressed interest in learning about spelling development and spelling instruction; to those whose spelling errors inadvertently provided me with grist for my analytical mill; and to Elinor Hartwig, my editor, who believed this book was needed.

CHAPTER 1

The Relationship Between Speech and Print

WHY IS KNOWLEDGE OF LANGUAGE NECESSARY?

I learned most of the content of this book long after my basic teacher training was completed. Knowing how to spell, it turned out, was not sufficient for knowing how to teach spelling or how to interpret the problems many of my students experienced. For me, as well as for most other literate people, knowledge of language had to be acquired through focused study. I learned that the structure of spoken and written language, and how words are represented in our alphabetic writing system, is essential for understanding how children learn to spell. Teaching language directly and explicitly to those who need help requires an intimate knowledge of word structure and how English orthography represents speech. After all, in our alphabetic system, spelling is word form written down, but few of us who teach or assess students have been asked to learn the details of word form, either spoken or written.

Teachers and clinicians must know their language intimately to address the specific confusions experienced by the person with spelling disability. Poor spellers typically are unable to analyze words into all of their sound segments or to recall the symbols that correspond to those segments. They need to be shown, explicitly, the structure of the written word and how it represents speech, and to be given ample practice writing words correctly. Students, even with significant learning disabilities, can make substantial gains when instruction is linguistically informed and systematic.

The literate teacher's tendency to conceptualize words as they are written, rather than spoken (Ehri 1994), must be overcome to understand speech-spelling correspondence. To illustrate: how many speech sounds are in the following words?

> **own   little   box   use   singing**

Own has two phonemes or speech sounds; *little* has four; *box* has four; and *singing* has five. In each case, the letters of the word do not correspond directly to the speech sounds that compose it. Furthermore, neither *balk* nor *chalk* has the speech sound /l/ in it; *pitch* has no /t/; and *yellow* has one /l/. These linguistic details are important because children who write *on*, *lidl*, *boks*, and *sigig* are spelling by phonemic analysis, writing one logical symbol for each sound they detect. To see that many misspellings are logical when a child is approaching spelling by speech sound analysis, we must differentiate between speech sounds and conventions of print.

English spelling is an indirect and complex rendering of speech, and there is often no direct, one-to-one correspondence between letters and speech sounds in English orthography. Not only are sound-symbol correspondences varied and complex, but also spelling represents meaningful segments and often contains information about a word's language of origin. Knowledge of the linguistics of spelling does not by itself resolve questions such as how the ability to spell develops in children, how students will respond to different types of instruction, or why spelling is impossibly difficult for some people, but it does provide the foundation for sensible and reliable observations of student behavior.

This book, therefore, begins with a brief lesson in linguistics. Because the following overview must be limited to essentials, the reader is encouraged to consult other language texts (Balmuth 1992; Fromkin and Rodman 1993; Hull 1985; Ladefoged 1982; Parker 1986), earlier theoretical work on language structure (C. Chomsky 1970; N. Chomsky and Halle 1968; Hanna et al. 1966; Venezky 1970) and current analyses of spelling (Henderson 1990; Henry 1988) on which I have relied heavily.

PHONETICS

The term **phonetics** refers to the identification and description of the speech sounds produced by speakers of a given language. Identification of the set of speech sounds or phonetic elements in English is more challenging than it might seem. The identity of English phonemes is sometimes ambiguous; the number is estimated to be between 44 (Hull 1985) and 52 (Hanna et al. 1966). Ambiguity arises from the fact that speech sounds are produced with variations in different phonemic contexts. Consider the medial consonant in *little* ; is it a /d/ or a /t/ or a composite of both?

One of the difficulties inherent in constructing the list of the speech sounds included in a language is that some "sounds," like the phonetic tongue flap [D] that occurs in *little*, are not phonemes. A **phoneme** is a distinctive unit that contrasts words like *tip* and *dip*, *ladder* and *latter*, although many phonemes can be pronounced in somewhat different ways, depending on the sounds that surround them. A **phonetic segment** is an articulatory gesture that exists in overt speech, such as the tongue flap [D]; in the case of *ladder* and *latter* the articulated tongue flap obscures the presumed identity of the underlying phoneme /t/ or /d/. If the word [læDr] was dictated to you, you would not know, without a context, whether you were to write *latter* or *ladder*. As Chomsky and Halle (1968) emphasized, the phoneme is an underlying abstract unit that may have several spoken forms (**allophones**). For example, most vowels can be "reduced" to an indistinct form called **schwa** (/ə/) in syllables that are unaccented. **Schwa** is not a **phoneme,** but a **phonetic variant** or **allophone** in words such as *a*lone, sof*a*, and d*e*cision. In addition, all the vowels in English are nasalized before nasal consonants /m/, /n/, and /ŋ/, but we do not extend the list of phonemes in English to include nasalized vowels, because they are not separate phonemes. To determine the list of speech sounds included in English, we have to be clear about whether we are interested in surface phonetic segments of speech, or in the abstract phonemes that constitute the underlying structure of the word.

Another difficulty in constructing the list of speech sounds contained in our language is that phonemes are not spoken as separated units. Rather, they are **coarticulated**, said together in a unit we call a syllable, and pronunciation of an individual phoneme is influenced by its neighbors. For example, the /p/ in *pit* is aspirated with a push of breath, but the /p/ in *spit* is not. The sounds in *word* are difficult to take apart, especially the vowel and the consonant /r/ that follows it. Each separate phoneme is not what it becomes in the undivided spoken syllable. Given this, no doubt, confusing introduction, let us consider the individual phonemes of English.

Consonants

Consonants are a class of speech sounds that are not vowels, and that are formed with either partial or complete obstruction of the air flow through the mouth. Although there is some disagreement among linguists as to what phonemes should be listed in the group of English consonants, in table 1 are a basic 25, plus five additional phonetic segments, with examples of English words that contain them.

Consonants are classified by linguists according to their place of articulation: the lips (**labial**) including /b/, /m/, and /p/; teeth (**dental**) including /f/ and /v/ and the forms of "th" /θ/ and /ð/; ridge behind the teeth (**alveolar**) including /d/, /t/, and /n/, /s/ and /z/, /l/ and /r/; hard palate or roof of the mouth (**palatal**) including /š/, /ž/, /ǰ/, /č/, and /j/; and soft palate or velum at the back of the mouth cavity (**velar**) including /k/, /g/, /ŋ/, /w/, and /ʍ/. The manner of articulation, how the air stream is affected as it travels through the mouth, is described by the terms **stop, nasal, fricative, affricate, glide,** and **liquid.** The reason for being familiar with the following chart (table 2) is that children's spelling errors often suggest that they discern certain featural similarities between or among phonemes.

Aspiration. Three of the voiceless stop consonants, /k/, /p/, and /t/, are aspirated at the beginnings of words or accented syllables in English, as signified by the superscript "h" in table 2. Aspiration involves a more forceful push of breath when the sound is produced in initial position than in final position. Say the words "top" and "spot" and put your hand up to your mouth to feel the difference in air pressure when the /t/ is enunciated in each position. The presence of aspiration does nothing to change the meaning of a

TABLE 1: PHONETIC SYMBOLS AND EXAMPLES OF SPELLINGS FOR CONSONANTS

Symbol[1]	*Examples*
p[h], p	*p*ick, *p*lace; sto*p*, a*pp*le
b	*b*at, *b*east, sta*b*, trou*b*le
m	*m*o*m*, co*mm*on, stu*m*p, bo*m*b
t[h], t	*t*ackle, ar*t*iculate; po*t*, s*t*ain, mess*ed*
d	*d*inner, *d*ress, ri*d*e, move*d*
n	*n*est, ski*n*, wi*nn*er, *mn*emonic, sig*n*, *kn*ight, *pn*eumatic
k[h], k	*k*iss, *qu*een, *c*ritic; sta*ck*, pi*c*nic, o*ch*re, ex*c*ite, criti*que*
g	*g*irl, a*g*ain, *gh*ost, *gu*ard, fin*g*er
ŋ	si*ng*, thi*n*k, fi*n*ger E*n*glish
f	*f*it, e*ff*ort, gra*ph*, tou*gh*
v	*v*ery, e*v*en, lo*v*e
s	*s*ap, mark*s*, a*ss*ess, *p*sychology, le*ss*, fan*c*y, fa*s*ten, a*s*cent, pie*ce*
z	*z*ip, bu*zz*, dog*s*, messe*s*, la*z*y, cra*z*e, lie*s*, *x*erox
θ	*th*ought, bo*th*, I*th*aca, Ma*tth*ew
ð	bo*th*er, *th*ough, mo*th*er, *th*e
š	*sh*ake, mu*sh*room, mi*ss*ion, ra*t*ion, gla*c*ial, *s*ugar
ž	vi*s*ion, a*z*ure, mea*s*ure
č	*ch*ase, ha*tch*, mu*ch*, na*t*ure, righ*t*eous
ǰ	*j*udge, villa*g*e, re*g*ion, *g*ist, gra*d*uate
l	*l*ady, fe*ll*, babb*le*
r	bi*r*d, *r*ace, singe*r*, ja*rr*ed
j	*y*ou, *u*se, f*eu*d, pla*y*ing
w	*w*itch, s*w*ear, se*w*er, q*u*ick
ʍ	*wh*ere, *wh*ich, *wh*ale
h	*h*appy, *h*ow, *wh*o, in*h*abit
ʔ	bo*tt*le, bu*tt*on (in some dialects)
D	li*tt*le, le*tt*er, la*dd*er, wri*t*er, ri*d*er

[1]The symbols chosen for this book are taken from Fromkin and Rodman, 1993, and include many from the International Phonetic Alphabet and others customarily used in the United States.

word; it happens automatically as a result of a phonological production rule that operates when we speak. While it may seem unnecessary to be concerned with such an articulatory subtlety, aspiration may cause a consonant to be easily distinguished during articulation, and therefore more likely to be noticed during the phonetic analysis that takes place during the act of spelling. Some consonants may be especially easy to detect because of articulatory features such as aspiration, and therefore they may be more likely to be spelled correctly. The absence of aspiration in final voiceless stop consonants (as in *mop* and *sick*) may be one reason why final consonants are harder for children to spell accurately than initial consonants.

    Obstruents and sonorants. The nonnasal stops (/p/, /t/, /k/, /b/, /d/, /g/), fricatives (/f/, /s/, /v/, /z/, /θ/, /ð/, /ž/), /š/ and affricates (/č/ and /ǰ/) form a major class of sounds because the air is fully or partially obstructed during articulation. These are the **obstruents**. **Sonorants** include those nasal and liquid sounds (/n/, /m/, /ŋ/, /l/, /r/) that resonate in the nasal passages or throat and can be pronounced continuously. They also include the glides (/h/, /w/, /y/). Glides are a unique group; they must always be followed by a vowel phoneme and are sometimes referred to as **semivowels**.

TABLE 2. CLASSIFICATION OF AMERICAN ENGLISH CONSONANTS BY PLACE AND MANNER OF ARTICULATION (AFTER FROMKIN AND RODMAN 1993)

	Bilabial	*Labiodental*	*Interdental*	*Alveolar*	*Palatal*	*Velar*	*Glottal*
Stop (oral)							
voiceless unaspirated	p			t		k	
voiceless aspirated	pʰ			tʰ		kʰ	
voiced	b			d		g	
Nasal (stop)	m			n		ŋ	
Fricative							
voiceless		f	θ	s	š		
voiced		v	ð	z	ž		
Affricate							
voiceless					č		
voiced					ǰ		
Glide							
voiceless						ʍ	h
voiced					j (y)	w	
Liquid				l			
				r			

TABLE 3. EXAMPLES OF VOICED/VOICELESS PHONEMES IN CONTRASTING PAIRS OF ENGLISH WORDS

Phoneme Pairs	Initial Position	Medial Position	Final Position
/p/, /b/	pin, bin	loppy, lobby	flap, flab
/t/, /d/	tin, din	writer, rider	mutt, mud
/k/, /g/	cot, got	echo, ego	smock, smog
/f/, /v/	fan, van	rifle, rival	leaf, leave
/θ/, /ð/	thigh, thy	ether, either	cloth, clothe
/s/, /z/	sip, zip	muscle, muzzle	fuss, fuzz
/š/, /ž/	—	mesher, measure	—
/č/, /ǰ/	chock, jock	lecher , ledger	rich, ridge

Voicing.   Note that there are eight pairs of consonants in English that differ only in voicing (see table 3). Each member of the pair is articulated in the same place and in the same manner as its partner, with the exception of voicing. Say the phoneme pairs aloud, and read aloud the pairs of words that exemplify the contrasts (notice also that spelling of the sounds may be somewhat deceptive). The voiced sounds are produced with a resonance in the throat that can be felt with the hand on the larynx or the hands placed over the ears.

Children's spelling errors may reflect insensitivity to the distinctive feature of consonant voicing, as in LEB[1] (leap), SIG (sick), or ARIF (arrive).

Nasality.   While it is obvious that /n/ and /m/ are nasal phonemes, because the sound produced is directed through the nose, and because the letter symbols we use for those sounds are predictable, the third nasal phoneme /ŋ/ is more elusive. This speech sound is produced in the same back-of-the-mouth (velar) position as /k/ and /g/, and often occurs before those consonants, as in *bank* and *finger*. The /ŋ/ is spelled two ways in English—with *ng* as in *sing, bang, hung,* and with an *n* alone as in *sink* and *English* [ɛ̧ŋglɪ̌s]. One of the reasons many people are not aware of the existence of /ŋ/ is that they believe, again because of spelling, that the *ng* spelling represents /n/ + /g/ and that each of the letters, instead of forming part of a digraph, represents a single speech sound. Another reason the identity of /ŋ/ may be elusive is that no word in English begins with that nasal sound. Some African words and names do—like Ngoro and Nkruma—but none does in English.

Syllabic consonants.   Four of the liquid and nasal consonants are sometimes employed in English as syllables. In words like *feather, rhythm, button,* and *little,* the final syllable does not have a vowel segment that is sep-

---

[1] Capital letters will be used throughout this book to represent children's inventive spellings or spelling errors.

arate and distinct from the consonant. In fact, the consonants /r/, /m/, /n/, and /l/, because they are sonorants, have both vowel and consonant features in word-final position. The spelling of *rhythm*, along with the suffix *-ism*, are unique instances in English of a syllable (/əm/) being spelled with no vowel letter. All other syllables in English are spelled with a vowel letter, even though in words like *little* the *e* is superfluous for the purposes of representing speech.

Vowels

Vowels are a class of speech sounds; a vowel must be in every English syllable, except for the instances of [əm] noted above, and forms the nucleus of the syllable. Consonants are formed around the vowel of the syllable. (The concept of the syllable can be illustrated if you try to sing a song without singing the vowels. It cannot be done, or done pleasingly, because the vowel is what singers sing and the throat must be open to allow the air to escape.) Vowels are classified according to whether the tongue is high or low in the mouth, and according to the part of the tongue—front or back—that is used.

Say the following sequence of words, exaggerating the vowels, while looking in a mirror: *beet, bit, bait, bet, bat, butt, bod(y), bore, boat, book, boot.* Notice how your mouth began in a closed, "smiley" position, then became open in the middle of the sequence, and by the last word had shifted to a rounded, closed position. Although you may have found it hard to detect, your tongue moved from a high, front position to a high, back position, while dropping down low in the middle of the sequence. (When the doctor wants to look in your throat, he asks you to say "ah"—the most middle, low, and open vowel). The phonetic symbols for the 15 vowel phonemes in English (after Fromkin and Rodman 1993) and examples of spellings for each vowel, are in table 4:

The position of these vowels in articulation is represented in figure 1. This figure also includes the "r-controlled" vowels, that change their identity when followed by /r/, and the spellings for the vowel blend /ju/, which some classification systems treat as a separate speech sound.

Tense and lax vowels. Most of the vowels can be classified as either tense or lax. The tense vowels include those we call "long" (as those in *beet, bait, boot,* and *boat*). Some systems classify /aj/ ("long i," as in *ice*) as a tense vowel (e.g., Hull 1985) and others classify it as a diphthong (Fromkin and Rodman 1993; Lindamood and Lindamood 1975). The tense vowels are produced with a slightly higher tongue position than the lax vowels, which include those we usually call "short" (like the vowels in *bid, bed, bad, body, and bud*).

TABLE 4. VOWEL PHONEMES OF ENGLISH, WITH COMMON SPELLINGS (from Fromkin and Rodman 1993)

/i/	seat, piece, remain, see, baby, coffey, impede, receive
/I/	bit, gym
/e/	bait, radar, say, neigh, great, state, vein
/ɛ/	instead, bed
/æ/	brat
/aj/	bite, might, silence, my, pie, hype
/a/	pot, father
/ʌ/	but
/ɔ/	author, walk, saw
/o/	boat, mobile, coke, snow, toe
/ʊ/	put, foot
/u/	scoop, drew, stupid. coupon
/ə/	(schwa) sofa, alone, television
/ɔj/	boy, toil
/aw/	ouch, shower

Lip rounding. All of the back vowels in English are formed with a rounding of the lips that is similar to the position of the mouth for the consonant /w/. There are no front, rounded vowels in English, although there are in other languages such as French (as in *bleu*).

Diphthongs. For our purposes, we will classify two English vowels as diphthongs, /ɔj/ and /aw/, as in *joy* and *house*. The "long i" vowel (/aj/) as in *ice* is not included as a diphthong because the diphthong quality varies according to the position of the vowel *(rival* vs. *pie)*, and because /aj/ is most commonly treated in phonics programs as a tense vowel, not a diphthong. Each of the vowels /ɔj/ and /aw/ is distinguished by having two phonetic segments. In /ɔj/, the tongue moves from low back position to high front position. In contrast, for the vowel in *mouse*, the tongue moves from low front position to high back position where the vowel must be rounded. In spite of the two phonetic segments in each vowel, the vowels are each unitary and distinct phonemes in English that do determine meaning. The existence of words such as *saw, so, soy,* and *sow* as separate lexical items in the language establishes the status of these vowels as phonemes, that is, as separate speech sounds.

Nasalization. Vowels, like consonants, can be produced nasally, by directing the flow of air through the nose. In English, however, nasalization of vowels only occurs by phonological rule and is not in itself critical to meaning. Whenever we pronounce a vowel in English before a nasal conso-

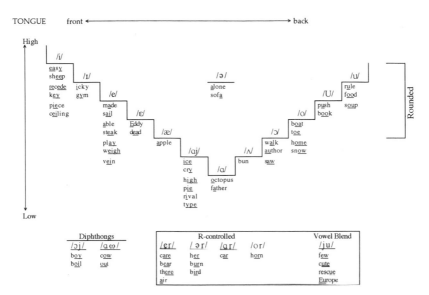

Figure I. Vowels and their Spelling by Place of Articulation.

nant, as in *bump, trunk,* or *anguish,* that vowel is automatically nasalized. Try pronouncing those words with your nose obstructed—as it would be if you had a bad cold—and the automatic nasalization will be obvious. Or pronounce these pairs of words as you hold your nose: *wet, went; bad, band; stop, stomp.*

PHONOLOGY

The term **phonology** is not equivalent to **phonetics** or **phonics.** It refers to the rule system employed when speech sounds are perceptually classified, combined into sequences, and uttered as sound patterns, as well as to the study of that rule system. Each language includes a system of constraints governing the order in which its speech sounds can be produced; moreover, these sequences are constrained by the limits of articulatory-motor production. The constraints operate more often within syllables than between them, determining not only the order permissible for phonemes but the position in which they can be spoken. For example, the consonant sequence [np] is not found within English syllables in any position; the sequence [mp] is never found at the beginnings of syllables but can exist after a vowel (*stump*) or across syllable boundaries (*impossible*).

The phonemes listed in tables 1 and 4 are really abstract classifications of many possible phonetic variations or segments that are found in the speech of individual language users. The mechanism by which our brains classify and identify phonemes is called **categorical perception.** Vowels, in particular, are subject to regional, dialectical, and individual variations in pronunciation that must be transcended by a listener. For example, Tennesseans hardly distinguish between *all* and *oil* ; Bostonians pronounce *park* like *pack*. What are the vowels in the words *daughter, walk*, and *ball*? Not everyone will agree that they are /ɔ/ as in *saw*; some people will argue that they are /a/ as in *cot*.

Not only is there a great deal of variety from speaker to speaker in how words and speech sounds are pronounced, which must be ignored as we categorize and interpret the acoustic input of speech, but the speech sounds that precede and follow a given phoneme in a word influence how these sounds are actually produced and create further variation in speech sound realization. Sometimes these differences lead to conflicting judgements regarding the phoneme constituents of a word. What is the vowel sound in *pink?* Ambiguities do not occur because the judgement of one speaker is right and that of another is wrong, but because phonemic perception is subject to individual variation. Vowels that are near each other in articulation (figure 1), as well as consonants that share overlapping features, are the most likely to provoke disagreement in our judgements of the phonemes that words contain.

Phonological Production Rules

Typically, we ignore certain subtle changes in pronunciation of phonemes that occur regularly by phonological rule when we are categorizing or identifying speech sounds. Many subtle changes occur automatically because of a phonological rule system that is learned unconsciously very early in language development. Vowel elongation, nasalization of vowels, flapping, and affrication of consonants /d/ and /t/ before /y/ are examples of these changes.

Vowel elongation.   Say the following groups of words:

write	ride
rice	rise
wife	wives
pipe	imbibe
smythe	writhe

You may have noticed that the vowel /aj/ in the second list has a longer duration or is "held out" longer than the vowel in the first list. The vowels in the second list are elongated and tend to have more of a diphthong or /i/ added to the end of the vowel. While we would identify all these vowels as "long i," their articulation differs by rule according to whether the consonant following the vowel is voiceless, as in the first list, or voiced, as in the second. This fact is relevant for understanding spelling in that the terms "long" and "short" for vowels as we use them in phonics have only a modest relationship to the reality of vowel duration in articulation. Children might be likely to spell an elongated /aj/ for instance as in *ride*, with a diphthong, as in RAED or RIYD, especially in words where the /aj/ is followed by a voiced consonant such as /d/.

Nasalization of vowels before nasal consonants. As mentioned previously, a vowel occurring before any of the three nasal consonants is automatically nasalized, in anticipation of that consonant. The features of one phoneme are "spread" or assimilated in the process of coarticulation with another adjacent phoneme. Note the phonetic transcription for the following words:

and	[æ̃nd]	add	[æd]
went	[wɛ̃nt]	wet	[wɛt]
gym	[ǰ̃ɪm]	gip	[ǰɪp]
gang	[gæ̃ŋ]	gag	[ḡæg]
bunk	[bʌ̃ŋk]	buck	[bʌk]

Only before the nasal consonant, in the left-hand list, is the vowel nasalized. Another problem arises with phonetic transcription of these words, which is the ambiguity of the nasal consonant itself. When the nasalization feature is "spread" to the vowel because of coarticulation, and the nasal consonant shares the same place of articulation as the following consonant, as with the velars /ŋk/ and the alveolars /n t/, the nasal consonant is "absorbed" by the phonemes around it. This phenomenon is particularly evident when the nasal occurs before a voiceless stop consonant (/t/, /p/, or /k/). As you say the words *wet* and *went*, notice that the segment /n/ is not clearly or separately articulated apart from the vowel and the final consonant. The phonetic reality of nasal deletion, particularly before voiceless stop consonants, is perceived by children when they learn to spell (Read 1986; Treiman 1993), and accounts for the very common practice of omitting the nasal letter before a stop consonant as in WAT (went), BOK (bonk) or JUP (jump).

Flapping. Consider the following list of words, and pronounce them naturally as if in the context of a phrase or sentence:

write	writer
ride	rider
let	letter
bet	better
lit	little, litter

If you were to say "writer" with a clear, aspirated /t/, you might seem affected, pretentious, or simply odd to your listener. Normally in American English, medial /t/ and /d/ phonemes are reduced by rule to a tongue flap [D] when they occur between an accented and an unaccented vowel. Thus, the word *attack* would not belong on the list of words with a medial flap, because the first vowel is unaccented and the last is stressed. The child who writes the word LIDL (little) again is giving a phonetically accurate transcription of the features in the word. The child who is asked to write [læDr] might write *latter* or *ladder* because either phonemic form could be "recovered" from the spoken word taken out of context.

Affrication of /t/ and /d/. In certain contexts, the alveolar consonants /t/ and /d/ are palatalized and are articulated much like the affricates /č/ and /ǰ/. Consider these word pairs: *task-trash; tend-trend; desk-dress; dagger-dragon,* and notice the change in the initial consonant before /r/ in the consonant blend. Children also notice this phenomenon and will portray the phonetic detail by writing words such as CHRAN (train) and JRAGN (dragon).

Further, when a /t/ or a /d/ occurs before the glide /j/, it is palatalized. Say these words and phrases:

A		**B**	
hit you	[hɪč ju]	hit me	[hɪt mi]
lead you	[lɨǰ ju]	lead me	[lid mi]
educate	[ɛǰjuket]	edify	[ɛdɪfaj]
graduate	[græǰjuet]	gradation	[gredešʌn]
infatuate	[ĭnfæčuet]	infantile	[ĭnfæntajl]

The phonetic alteration of /t/ and /d/ in column A is predictable and regular because it always occurs in the same phonemic environment before the glide /j/. Note that the single letter *u* in the last three words in column A represents two phonemes or phonetic segments, /j/ and /u/, as in the difference betwen *use* and *ooze*. The spellings of words with this phonological complexity can be difficult for children to spell, because they exemplify a more general problem with English spelling, the indirect relationship between alphabetic orthography and articulatory phonetics.

Syllabication   While it is easy enough to say that words such as *petal, little, better, rhythm, addict* and *comment* have two syllables, each with a vowel nucleus, the phonological division between the syllables in these words is ambiguous. One cannot tell, unequivocally, where these words divide naturally into units of sound, because the medial consonant between the two vowels can be associated with the first or second syllables. However, the predictable spellings of certain syllable types do help the student of spelling, who cannot rely on pronunciation alone to resolve whether there should be a doubled consonant present in the word.

One or more of the syllables in each content word (as opposed to function words such as articles *a* and *the*) is stressed. Sometimes stress determines meaning, as in the noun-verb stress alternation of cóntent - contént, cónflict - conflíct, ímpact - impáct, pérvert - pervért. In addition, compound words in English have a distinctive stress pattern. Consider *houseboat, blackbird, lighthouse, crackpot, backwater:* The first syllable is stressed in all, allowing contrast in some instances with the same words in non-compound form, such as *black bird.* Thus a linguistically sensitive learner probably uses the phonological cue of the stress to identify compounds. The fact that *already, himself* and *myself* depart from this pattern may add to compounds' ambiguity for spelling. The persistent difficulty of compounds for learners with disabilities may be rooted in their insensitivity to phonological information, and their inability to make use of stress cues.

Summary.   The term **phonology** refers to the rule system constraining sequences of phonemes and their production, psycholinguistic phenomena affecting speech perception such as categorical perception of phonemes, the processes governing articulation of phonemes, and other dimensions of the sound system of the language, including stress, tonality, and phrase contour. Understanding phonology is important for understanding spelling. Because our alphabetic writing system is designed, at least in part, to represent the sounds of language, children's spelling attempts often express what they know and believe about the speech sounds in words.

MORPHOLOGY

The term **morphology** does not refer to grave digging, as a student once surmised, but to the smallest *meaningful* units of language. *Morphe* is a Greek root meaning "form." A single word may contain one or more morphemes, as in *sex* (1), *sexy* (2), *unsexy* (3), and - possibly - *unsexiest* (4). A word may be made up of a single morpheme with more than one syllable, as in *corduroy, fahrenheit*, and *Mississippi.* Morphemes may be **bound** or **free**. If a morpheme is free it can stand alone; if it is bound, it must exist in combination with other morphemes and cannot be a word by itself. Prefixes, suffixes, and some roots that cannot stand alone are bound morphemes, such as the *-ology* in *psychology* and the *peri-* in *perimeter.*

Inflectional morphemes are those grammatical endings that do not change the root of the word but that signify possession, gender, or number if the word is a noun (John*'s*, trap*s*, bench*es*); tense, voice, or mood if the word is a verb (snapp*ed*, giv*en*, sing*ing*); or comparison, if the root is an adjective (strang*er*, strang*est*). Inflections are usually unaccented or, in the case of the past tense *-ed*, not even pronounced as a syllable (*burned; pitched*) which adds to their difficulty for spelling.

Derivational morphemes often do change the part of speech of the root and are referred to as **prefixes** and **suffixes** in language arts instruction. They include a large set of meaningful word parts that are used in combination with others to form new words. Many of these in English were originally borrowed from Greek and Latin (Balmuth 1992; Henry 1988). While their spellings may be quite consistent, their influence on meaning may be somewhat obtuse or constrained. For example, *matchless* and *peerless* refer to a superlative condition, not simply a condition of being without. Derivational rules act unpredictably; *-ment* is often added to verbs to create nouns (*enjoyment, deferment, employment*) but it cannot be added to every verb. Derivational morphemes are usually spelled consistently even though their meaning or pronunciation may change according to the morphemes with which they are combined. More will be said later about this important aspect of English spelling.

ENGLISH ORTHOGRAPHY

A theoretical and empirical basis for understanding English orthography has been well established since the late 1960s (Chomsky 1970; Chomsky and Halle 1968; Hanna, Hodges, and Hanna 1971; Venezky 1967). Many linguistic analyses have made the case that English is far from just an imperfect system for transcribing speech, as spelling reformers have repeatedly claimed. Rather, it is a system that represents phonology through a complex mapping of letters to sounds, and that simultaneously represents meaningful units. Thus it is often described as **morphophonemic.** Chomsky and Halle (1968) and C. Chomsky (1970) even described English as an optimal system for representing both sound and meaning. Some of the words in English that do not correspond directly to sound, such as *bomb, sign,* and *hymn* can be pronounced by application of a phonological deletion rule applied to the related forms *bombard, signal,* and *hymnal;* the spelling system, by spelling the lexical root consistently, preserves the meaningful relationship between the words even though the pronunciation of related forms changes. English is replete with examples of spelling that preserves meaningful roots in spite of changes in pronunciation from one form of a word to another, such as *press - pressure; compete - competition; theater - theatrical; magic - magician; human - humanity.*

How faithfully does the English spelling system represent speech sounds, however? A definitive analysis of this question was performed in 1966 by Hanna, Hanna, Hodges, and Rudorf, who took the 17,000 most often used words in English print, and analyzed them by computer for sound-symbol regularities. In contrast to a perfect or ideal phonetic transcription of speech, which might have one letter for each speech sound, English uses over 170 graphemes to spell the limited set of 42 phonemes (they classified 52 phonemes, including r-controlled variations). Letter configurations such as *oa-e,igh, ough, eau,* and *tch* are graphemes because they spell or correspond to one speech sound or phoneme. Obviously, most graphemes in English are more than one letter if 170 spellings can be created with 26 letter symbols. Note that the concept of a multiletter grapheme corresponding to a phoneme is somewhat different from the idea of "sounded" and "silent" letters in words. Although many graphemes have unsounded letters, the important concept is that the letter groups form a stable configuration that corresponds to a speech sound in a predictable manner, and most "silent" letters are part of these stable configurations used in discrete sets of words. Venezky (1970) termed these elements "relational units" for spelling. It is descriptively accurate, for example, to say that both *tch* and *ch* are spellings for /č/. One is as arbitrary as the other in terms of the symbolization process, and both are units that must be learned for spelling.

Hanna et al. (1966) demonstrated that at least twenty phonemes had grapheme spellings that were over 90% predictable, and 10 others were predictable over 80% of the time. Vowels collectively were less consistent than consonants. Only eight phonemes had individual predictability of less than 78%, and five of these were vowels.

Predictability, however, was not a straightforward issue. Predictability of most phoneme-grapheme relationships was improved after taking into consideration several major constraints that operate to govern correspondences in English. The predictability of many graphemes depended upon the position of the phoneme in the syllable—initial, medial, or final—and often on the phoneme environment in which that sound occurred. Furthermore, the stress of the syllable often determined the preferred spelling for a phoneme.

To illustrate, there are four common ways to spell /k/: *c, k, ck, ch.* In addition, the letter combination *qu* is redundant for /kw/, and the letter *x* represents a sound combination, /ks/. Predictability of complex correspondences such as the spellings for /k/ is increased when the position of the sound in the syllable and the consideration of the sounds that precede or follow it are taken into account. At the end of a syllable following a short vowel, *ck* is the preferred spelling for /k/ (po*ck*et, bu*ck*le, wi*ck*er). The *qu* combination always occurs at the beginnings of syllables (*qu*it). Other spellings for /k/ depend on the phoneme environment in which the sound occurs as well as its position in the syllable. Whether the letter *k* or *c* is used to spell /k/ at the beginnings of syllables depends on the letter or phoneme that follows it: when /k/ is followed by vowels spelled with *a, o,* or *u,* the letter *c* is used (*cat, cushion, cozy*); when /k/ is followed by vowel letters *i* or *e,* the letter *k* is used, as in *kite, ketchup, keen.* In consonant blends, /k/ followed by /r/ or /l/ is always spelled with a *c* (*clean, crazy*). To add one more layer of complexity, word origin also determines spelling: ch for /k/ is used almost exclusively in words of Greek origin such as *chorus* and *orchestra.*

The complexity of sound-symbol correspondence can also be illustrated with the vowel /o/. Clearly, Vice President Dan Quayle was unaware of these constraints when he failed to recall the spelling of *potato,* but not many people have this information at their fingertips. According to Hanna et al. (1966), only two words in English with unaccented final syllables ending with /o/ spell it with *oe, mistletoe* and *oboe.* In contrast, 1,084 words with /o/ in syllable-final position spell it with plain *o.* When /o/ ends a word and is accented, however, the preferred spelling is *ow,* as in *blow, below, tow, snow.* Just for good measure, it is also interesting to note that when /t/ and /d/ follow an /o/, the preferred spelling is *oa* (*boat, float, goad, load*), but otherwise, /o/ in the middle of accented syllables that end words is most often spelled *o-e* (*abode, enclose, alone*).

What use is this sort of information? Whether and how to teach sound-symbol relationships in spelling will be dealt with in a later chapter, but at the very least, Hanna et al. established that English is a predictable and rule-based spelling system with layers of constraints governing correspondences, including position, stress, and phoneme environment. Given only the sound-symbol algorithm they generated from their corpus of 17, 000 words, 50% of the vocabulary could be spelled with no errors, and another 36% could be spelled with one error. Only 14% of the words were "irregular" in that the sound-symbol agorithm spelled them with two or more errors. In a retrospective analysis of the spelling errors made by the sound-symbol algorithm, the authors also determined that if morphological representation in spelling were taken into account, many more words could be spelled correctly. Morphological elements of significance included compound forms, such as *caretaker* and *playfellow,* whose spellings would be, by rule, *cartaecer* and *plafelo* if the sound-symbol algorithm were relied on exclusively; words with affix-root structure like *complicated* and *abbreviation* spelled *complicaeted* and *abreviation* by the algorithm; and various "word families" such as those that use *igh* for /aj/ , those that double *f, l,* and *s* at the ends of one-syllable words (*mall, staff, hiss*), and those that use the *old, ild* patterns. In addition, the sound-symbol correspondence algorithm alone had no way to adjust for words following foreign language spelling patterns, such as *chaise, buffet, beige, croquet,* and *machete.*

What were the words spelled with three or more errors, those that might be considered "unpredictable" by sound-symbol correspondence rules? Many were compounds, affixed forms, or foreign words. Many were words of Latin or Greek derivation such as *philosophize, psychology, semicircular, officiate, schizophrenia, polysyllabic,* and *accommodating,* that could be spelled based on knowledge of morphology and word origin. And many were high frequency, old words that have retained "odd" spellings from their early Anglo-Saxon origins, including *said, does, were, who, one, two, their, lose, gone, done.* Horn (1969) once surmised that 354 of the 500 most often used words in writing were to some degree irregular in English, most of those from Anglo-Saxon.

Orthographic Rules

In addition to the sound-symbol rule system, the orthography itself embodies constraints on permissible letter sequences and letter uses (Venezky 1967). Some letters in English can never be doubled within a syllable or between syllables such as *j, y, i* (exception, *skiing*), *k* (exception, *bookkeeper*). Consonant digraphs (*sh, th, wh, ch, sh, ng, ph, gh*) act as relational units and spell single speech sounds; they also cannot be doubled. A doubled consonant or its substitute must intervene between a stressed short vowel syllable and an inflected ending beginning with a vowel. Thus, the complex spellings *ck, dg, tch,* and *x* replace doubled consonants after short or lax vowels, in words such as *picnicking, dodger, pitching,* and *boxer.* (Exceptions to the *tch* generalization: *much, rich, which, such, bachelor*).

Some letters in English are never used in word-final position, particularly *j* and *v.* Thus, the permissible spellings for word-final [j] are *dge* and *ge.* In words ending with [v] such as *love, have, seive, live, dove, leave,* and *salve,* the marker *e* is placed at the end of the word so that it does not violate the "v" rule, regardless of the pronunciation of the vowel. In this way, then, all the "v" words are predictable, not according to sound-symbol correspondence necessarily, but according to orthographic rule.

There are other roles for the marker "e" in English spelling, which is the most often used letter in the language (Venezky 1970). The letter "e" indicates when a vowel is long as in *nape* and *rode.* It also indicates when a "c" or a "g" should have its "soft" sound, as in *page, piece,* and *price.* Further, it keeps some words from looking like plurals (*please,* not *pleas*; *horse,* not *hors*; *mouse,* not *mous*).

Some spelling patterns in English work at the level of the syllable. Each syllable must have a vowel letter, even when syllabic consonants are "carrying" the vowel. A name like CVRTLIK, which has three syllables, is obviously not of English origin for that reason. English has six basic syllable spelling patterns that are useful to know because they often explain why words are spelled as they are (see table 5).

TABLE 5. SIX SYLLABLE STRUCTURES IN ENGLISH SPELLING

Syllable Type	Examples	Explanation
Closed	rabbit, comment napkin, picnic exact, racket	These syllables contain a short vowel followed by a consonant. In a multisyllable word, a short vowel is usually protected from an adjacent vowel by two consonants.
Open	*mo*ment, *ra*dar *mu*tation, *de*cide	The long vowel in an open syllable is usually separated from the next syllable with only one consonant letter or no consonant, because an open syllable ends with a vowel.
R-Controlled	bird, berth port, absurd	When a vowel is followed by /r/, the vowel often loses its identity as long or short, and is coarticulated with the /r/.
Vowel Team	great, trawl afloat, explain	Many vowels are spelled with two adjacent vowel letters, such as ai, ay, ee, ea, oi, oy, oa, au, aw, ew, ue, oo, ie and ei. Vowel teams may represent long, short, or diphthong vowels; they may be followed by consonants or used at the ends of syllables.
Vowel-Silent E	com*pete*, de*cide* a*bate*ment	These syllables spell long vowels with a vowel-consonant silent-e pattern.
Consonant-le	table, bugle babble, little rifle, whiffle	When syllabic /l/ occurs at the end of a spoken word it most often is preceded by a consonant that is part of that syllable. For example, *bugle* has an open first syllable, but *little* has a closed first syllable. The nature of the preceding vowel will determine if a doubled consonant is needed before the consonant-le.

Ending rules.   There are three major orthographic rules that govern addition of endings onto words of certain syllable types. They are much easier to learn and teach if the above syllable types are already understood (see table 6).

TABLE 6. ORTHOGRAPHIC CHANGE RULES FOR ADDING ENDINGS

Examples	*Rule*
run, running bat, batter wet, wettest	**Consonant Doubling**. When a one-syllable word with one vowel ends in one consonant, double the final consonant before adding a suffix beginning with a vowel.
confer, conferring occur, occurred open, opening	**Advanced Consonant Doubling.** When a word has more than one syllable, double the final consonant when adding an ending beginning with a vowel, if the final syllable is accented and has one vowel followed by one consonant.
confine, confining waste, wasteful extreme, extremely	**Drop Silent E**. When a root word ends in a silent *e*, drop the *e* when adding a suffix beginning with a vowel. Keep the *e* before a suffix beginning with a consonant.
study, studying studious beauty, beautiful	**Change Y Rule**. When a root word ends in a *y* preceded by a consonant change *y* to *i* before a suffix, except *ing*. If the root word ends in a *y* preceded by a vowel, just add the suffix.

SUMMARY

The spelling patterns of English are predictable and logical if one takes into account several major layers of language represented in the orthography. The many factors that determine predictability in spelling include sound-symbol correspondences, syllable patterns, orthographic rules, word meaning, word derivation, and word origin. Predictability is not an either/or proposition, and it would be erroneous to try to classify English vocabulary in a dichotomous fashion. Only a few correspondences work all the time regardless of sound sequence, in words such as *that, must* and *pan*. Other correspondences are predictable but determined by position of a phoneme in a word, syllable stress, and phonemic environment. These are the *conditional* or *variant* predictabilities, which are much more common than the invariant correspondence patterns. Correspondences can be predictable and frequent; they characterize a large set of spellings in the vocabulary. Others are predictable but infrequent; they belong to a limited, but distinctive "family" of words that share a spelling pattern, such as the group including *find, blind, kind, rind, hind, mind*. Odd and truly unpredictable spellings, such as *of, aunt,* and *does,* are only a small percentage of English, mostly leftovers from our Anglo-Saxon heritage, although those words are overrepresented among the words most often used for writing. Finally, spelling often preserves and visually represents meaningful word parts and meaningful relationships between words, and often reflects the language from which a word originated.

Given these facts about our written language, the questions might then be asked, how do children learn about spelling? What is the predictable course of spelling development? What sensitivities do children bring to the task of learning to spell, and how much do natural abilities account for learning to spell in contrast to deliberate acquisition of information through study and practice? How do children who spell poorly differ from those who spell well? What can be done to help them?

RECOMMENDED FOR FURTHER READING

Balmuth, M. 1992. *The Roots of Phonics*. Baltimore: York Press.

This book succeeds in providing a clear, scholarly, concise and interesting history of English phonics. It discusses the evolution of our sound-symbol system over many centuries, and explains why our modern language is spelled the way it is.

Bryson, B. 1990. *The Mother Tongue: English and How It Got That Way*. New York: Avon.

Although only one chapter is explicitly about spelling, this delightful book can satisfy any language lover's appetite for knowledge about the historical development of English vocabulary, grammar, writing conventions, and usage.

Fromkin, V., and Rodman, R. 1993. *An Introduction to Language*. New York: Holt, Rinehart.

This basic linguistics text is comprehensive and scholarly, but readable. In its chapters on phonetics, phonology, and morphology, it includes many examples not only from English but also from other languages to illustrate concepts. It does not emphasize the structure of written language as much as the structure of spoken language.

Hull, M. 1985. *Phonics for the Teacher of Reading,* 4th Edition. Columbus: Charles E. Merrill.

This self-paced, programmed instruction text provides a useful course of study for the teacher who is unfamiliar with the common vowel and consonant spellings in English. This book is limited to sound-symbol correspondences, and does not discuss morphology and its relationship to English spelling.

Parker, F. 1986. *Linguistics for Non-linguists*. Boston: College-Hill.

An excellent introductory text on language structure and language acquisition that can be understood by a person with little previous background knowledge.

CHAPTER 2

Mental Processes in Spelling

WHAT'S IN A THEORY?

Our theoretical view of the mental processes involved in spelling will guide our approach to instruction and affect our interpretation of spelling behavior. Each theory summarized here attempts to explain the nature of the mental processes used in spelling and the relative contribution that those processes make to the production of written words. Questions of interest to cognitive neuropsychologists and psycholinguists who construct theoretical models of spelling include: Does the brain have several different pathways available to it for spelling production? What are those pathways specialized to do? Do individuals differ in the extent to which they rely on different mental circuitry or neural pathways to spell? What do the effects of brain damage tell us about normal spelling processes? How do the components of the spelling system interact with one another? Do the mental processes employed during spelling depend on a person's stage of spelling development? Models that address such questions help us understand individual differences in spelling skill, individual responses to instruction, and the advantages and disadvantages of certain teaching strategies.

It is relevant to know, for example, the extent to which a literate adult relies on a kind of subvocalization process or internal representation of speech in order to spell. If most adults write words through a "direct route" from a visual image of the whole word to its written representation, then phonological recoding or mental translation of a word into its spoken form might not be necessary for successful spelling in the person who is already literate. One might then be tempted to argue that spelling should be taught to novices by whole word memorization, rather than by sound-symbol correspondence. The evidence for and against that presupposition should be carefully considered, as its truth or falsehood could affect the design of an entire reading and spelling curriculum. In addition, it is important to know if the processes employed to spell predictable words like *mandate* and *cameo,* homophones like *their* and *there,* and irregular words such as *of, said,* and *once* are similar or different. How should these word categories be treated in instruction?

COGNITIVE ANALYSES OF SPELLING PROCESSES IN ADULTS

The mental mechanisms employed when adults spell have been inferred from experimental studies of literate people, naturalistic studies of "normal" spelling errors and slips of the pen, and meticulous case study analyses of individuals with brain lesions. Currently there are two primary competing models of the cognitive processes involved in spelling. One, *dual-route theory,* proposes that there are two separate neural pathways that can be employed to spell and that these pathways are linked but can be dissociated. The other, *connectionist* theory, emphasizes the extent to which different aspects of word knowledge are tapped simultaneously and in parallel when spelling occurs, and also emphasizes the interdependence of one type of linguistic knowledge on another.

Dual-Route Theory

Many cognitive neuropsychologists, particularly of a British school of neuropsychology, have presented evidence from both laboratory experiments and accidents of nature for a dual-route theory of reading and spelling (Ellis 1993; Frith 1980a; Stuart and Coltheart 1988). The models they have generated depict an information-processing system in which different aspects of word knowledge are stored in separate locations in the neural network underlying written language production. Called modules, these sites of information storage are connected by communication pathways that can operate independently of one another, like circuits in a switchboard. In many cases of acquired brain dysfunction, selective impairment of specific components of the communication system appears to have occurred, resulting in impairment of one of the key information storage modules or impairment of the pathways that connect them.

It has been proposed that information about the sound structure of words is stored in a **phonological** module, while information about the letters in printed words is stored in a **visual-orthographic** module. The brain establishes two independent routes from a meaning processor to spell (or read) a word. The first is a phonological route, the second a visual-orthographic route (see figure 2).

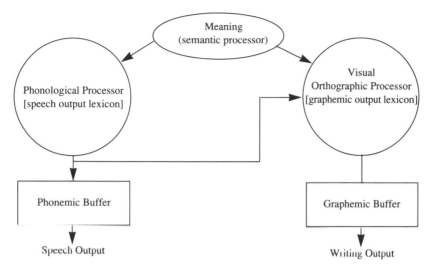

Figure 2. A simple model of the processing components of spelling production (after Ellis 1993).

The visual-orthographic module, termed the *graphemic output lexicon* in Ellis's (1993) schematic model of spelling processes, is the storehouse of words whose spellings have been memorized. The storehouse holds *any* learned word, no matter what its degree of predictability. This storehouse of written word knowledge is connected to both the semantic or meaning module, and to the phonological module or *speech output lexicon* in Ellis's terminology. The spelling of a particular word can be retrieved from the visual-orthographic processor and produced in response to a meaning cue and/or a pronunciation cue. If a meaning cue alone triggers the recall of a visual-orthographic memory of a word, without a pronunciation or phonological cue, a mistake might arise and a word of similar meaning but different sound form may be written, as in *little* for *small*. If the retrieval of a word from orthographic memory is triggered by a sound cue without full connection with a meaning cue, a homophone might be written, as in *to* for *two*, or *ate* for *eight*. If the retrieval of a word from orthographic memory is stimulated by a partial or degraded phonological cue, a word with similar but slightly different phonemic structure might be written, as in *rich* for *ridge*. And if the letters of a word are not completely known, a visually similar word might be retrieved from the orthographic processor with letters omitted or rearranged (*wuold/ would*). All these examples typify "slips of the pen" that adults make who already know the spellings of many words, and that can be explained with a dual-route model of spelling processes.

The graphemic knowledge (knowledge of letter strings) stored in the visual-orthographic processor is abstract and convertible into various forms or representations. The visual-orthographic image of a word may be expressed in lower case letters, upper case letters, manuscript or cursive; it may be typed or it may be spelled orally. We do not necessarily remember a word in one form or another, but we do remember a string of letter identities that can be expressed in several ways. Different output pathways, however, are employed in oral spelling, typing, and handwriting, and it is possible for any of those pathways to operate successfully even if one of the others is non-functional. For example, people who have lost the use of their hands can spell aloud; people who have lost the use of their speech may be able to type.

In the phonological processor, or speech output lexicon (Ellis's terminology), words are remembered in their spoken form as sequences of speech sounds. The phonological processor also includes a specific function of working verbal memory that allows words to be analyzed into their separate speech sounds for mapping to graphemes. Knowledge of the most common graphemes or spellings for each speech sound or syllable pattern is established in the phonological module. The phonological processor allows us to spell words not already known or retrievable from the visual-orthographic word store. Relying on this module, one can transcribe a spoken word (real or nonsense) by identifying the speech sounds and generating reasonable letter spellings for those sounds, without knowing how the word is spelled by convention. The result is phonetically accurate spelling that may not look like the target word (*ankshous/anxious*).

In spite of the adult's ability to recall whole words automatically, with minimal phonemic recoding during spelling, phonemic representations do play a part in retrieval of memorized words. Accurate phonemic coding is necessary to retrieve accurate spellings from graphemic memory. If the phonological image is inaccurate, for example if similar speech sounds are not completely discriminated or identified, mistakes such as *sog* for *sock* can arise. The phonological route becomes involved as well when the spelling of an irregular word is forgotten, but a phonetic translation such as "wed-nes-day" (Wednesday) is employed to prompt recall of the letters. In addition, the phonological route is employed as a check on the output generated from graphemic memory, and is the device by which missing letters or syllables are detected (e.g., *rember*/remember).

The phonological processor is responsible for learning and storing possible spellings for phonemes and phoneme combinations. However, it makes use of all the information available in the graphemic processor to accomplish the construction of the phoneme-grapheme links. When we assemble the spellings of unknown words using phoneme-grapheme mappings, our choices for spellings are influenced by our knowledge of which spellings are most likely in our writing system. For example, if asked to spell the nonsense word "brame," we are likely to write *brame* or *braim*. Although we might know words like *skein* and *weight,* we would be highly unlikely to choose the low-probability spelling *ei* for the "long a" vowel. Our choice of *aim* or *ame* would reflect our knowledge of the most likely orthographic patterns in text. In addition, our choice of the higher probability spellings could be influenced by priming, that is immediate prior exposure to a word with one or the other pattern, which would increase the likelihood that we would choose the pattern most recently activated in memory.

Results of priming experiments conclusively demonstrate that the phonological processor and graphemic processor normally interact with each other, and that assembly of unknown or nonsense words via the phonological route draws on as much orthographic knowledge as it can access. Conversely, it is likely that phonological images of words in the phonological processor are influenced by orthographic knowledge. People do come to believe that words are pronounced a certain way or that they have certain speech sounds in them because of their spellings (Ehri 1986). For example, many adults do believe that *pitch* contains one more phoneme than *rich* because of the extra *t* in the first word.

Application of dual-route theory in understanding the effects of brain dysfunction. Dual-route theory emphasizes that there are cognitive processes employed in phoneme-grapheme association and word generation that are distinct and separable from whole word memorization, and that pathways linking the modules of written word memory are separate. Much of this evidence comes from adult case studies of individuals with acquired brain dysfunction that has very localized and specific effects. It has been demonstrated in neurologically impaired adults that individuals may suffer selected impairment of the phonological and visual-orthographic pathways for word production. Adults with acquired lesions have been known to retain the ability to spell previously learned, real words, but to lose almost completely the ability to generate a novel, phonetically accurate spelling of a nonsense word (Shallice 1981). Consequently, Ellis (1993) and other cognitive neuropsychologists have argued that learned words must be stored in a graphemic word production mechanism that is separate from the phonological system. This module can operate independently of the phoneme-grapheme production system and can continue to function even if the phonological module is impaired. A meaning cue alone can prompt retrieval of known words from the visual-orthographic store.

If the phonological processor and the semantic processor are disconnected from the orthographic processor, a "deep dysgraphia" syndrome may result. Analogous to what British neuropsychologists have labeled "deep dyslexia," the affected person can produce whole words from dictation, but cannot spell nonsense or novel words through the sound-symbol recoding route. In addition, concrete words (*table, lunch*) are often spelled better than abstract ones (*ominous, famous*) and content words better than function words. When words are dictated, the patient will often write a semantically related word that is phonemically distant from the target, such as *flower* for *bloom, chair* for *table,* and *kid* for *child.*

In contrast, if the graphemic processing module is selectively impaired, the individual will be dependent upon phoneme-grapheme assembly processes to spell both new and previously learned words, which no longer can be recalled. This type of impairment has been termed "surface dysgraphia," analogous to "surface dyslexia." There may be some retention of high frequency or overlearned sight words, and partial memory for letter sequences or letter patterns. However, recall of the spelling of homophones is almost impossible for people with surface dysgraphia, because the meaning processor is disconnected from the visual-orthographic store, and these individuals are most likely to use the most frequent or common sound-symbol spellings when little is recalled about a word.

Are the word memories used for reading recognition and those used for spelling recall stored in different memory systems? The likelihood that this is the case, as argued by Ellis (1993), is demonstrated by the fact that adults can read and write simultaneously, as well as the fact that reading and spelling can be selectively impaired in brain-damaged adults. Further, one can read on the basis of a partial word-matching process, whereas spelling requires a much more explicit and detailed recall of letter sequences (Frith and Frith 1983).

Connectionist Models

Connectionist models of reading and spelling processes are newer than dual-route models and were generated in reaction to some of the problems evident in dual-route theory (Adams 1990; Seidenberg and McClelland 1989; Van Orden, Pennington, and Stone 1990). Connectionist models emphasize that language learning depends on the extraction and recall of *relationships* among events or phenomena. All relevant knowledge is activated in memory when a word is spelled, for example, and various aspects of word knowledge interact with and influence one another constantly.

Connectionist models, like dual-route models, pose that there are separate processors (i.e., separate neural systems) responsible for storage and retrieval of phonological, orthographic, and semantic information as reading and writing are carried out. Within each of these processors, neural connections between simple units or building blocks have been made and strengthened through exposure and use. The links between bits of information such as phonemes and graphemes are weighted or strengthened as exposure to and practice using the links occurs. The stronger a connection (the greater the association weight), the easier and faster the association is retrieved. The corpus of words already known to the person, as well as that person's experience with these words, determines the association weights between sounds and symbols that may exist in his or her memory at any one time. Thus, the most common words that are frequently used in a person's writing would be recalled most easily.

Connection weights are established between sounds and the spellings that can be used for most of them. Stronger weights would be established between written and spoken words that are very frequent, that have a commonly used spelling pattern, or that a person has practiced. The fact that an average person asked to spell "brame" would chose *brame* or *braim,* not *breighm,* is a function of the connection weights that exist for "long a" spellings. These have been acquired through direct experience with multiple examples of the most frequent spellings for /e/, and may have been facilitated with direct instruction.

When Treiman (1993) analyzed all of the spellings generated by a first-grade class over a year, she documented that in misspelled words containing consonant digraphs, the initial consonants (*s* in *sh*; *t* in *th*, etc.) were written far more often than the *h* or some other letters. According to connectionist theory, the initial consonants were the more heavily weighted of the two letters in the memories of the first graders, although they did not represent speech directly. Misspellings for /d/ were about equally *b* and *t*, showing that the visual and phonological features of *d* were about equally weighted.

When a word is spelled, all aspects of word knowledge stored in the different processors are activated and used. The processors, although separate knowledge banks, share information during production of words. If phonological analysis is not required because the visual-orthographic word store already "knows" the word and can generate it as a whole letter string, the phonological processor may simply serve to monitor the plausibility of what is produced. If graphemic memory is incomplete, knowledge of spelling patterns in the phonological processor is employed to generate a plausible word, using whatever unit of analysis is necessary: syllable, rime, or phoneme. Individual sound-symbol connections have been amalgamated into larger units when redundancy in the writing system fosters the building of strong connections between letter groups that are often used to spell rimes or syllables. According to connectionist models, people know that the "ack" syllable uses a *ck* for /k/ not because they have learned a rule, but because they have used this pattern in writing and seen this pattern in print so many times that the connection weight between final /k/ after short vowels and the *ck* spelling is very strong.

Rather than emphasizing the separateness of processing routes, connectionist theory emphasizes the importance of each linguistic processor for facilitating the growth and use of the others. In most people, all three processing modules are basically intact and work in concert. Connectionism also suggests that individual differences in spelling ability are attributable primarily to the strength and clarity of phonological images in the phonological processor and to the explicitness and completeness of images in the orthographic processor. Pupils with weaknesses in phoneme detection in turn have trouble with sound-symbol learning. The speech template onto which correct letter associations can be "hooked" is insufficiently differentiated for those connections to become strong. Inefficiencies or problems with speech processing restrict or distort the information being fed to the graphemic processor.

Linnea Ehri's Amalgamation Theory

Ehri (1986, 1987, 1989, 1994) who has conducted both naturalistic observations and many laboratory experiments of reading and spelling acquisition, emphasizes the degree to which spelling and reading are associated, and the close interconnectedness between various aspects of word knowledge. She proposes that several kinds of knowledge are necessary for spelling, and that these develop reciprocally, one influencing the other. Word identities in mature, literate persons have several "unitized" or "amalgamated" identities, including phonological, morphological, orthographic, semantic, and syntactic features. These features in fact become so strongly bonded when learned that individuals will base their beliefs about words on their knowledge of spelling rather than their knowledge of pronunciation. Fourth-grade children who can spell will perceive an extra syllable in words such as *family, different,* and *comfortable* more easily than those who cannot spell. Letters are more easily remembered when they correspond to sound than when they are silent, as in *listen.* Sound segmentation becomes easier when letters are used to help children conceptualize those sounds. Children learn about language structure through print. For example, they learn to distinguish short vowels from each other, and which phonetic features to ignore in spelling, like the shift of /ɛ/ toward /e/ in *egg.* Children in the early grades do not pay attention to morphology, and learn about it through exposure to print. Often they are not aware that words are separate until they see them in writing. Children who can spell are quicker to detect rhyme in words like *ear* and *spear* with spellings similar to each other than they are to detect rhyme in words like *hair* and *spare.* Ehri suggests that children who spell poorly demonstrate much more separateness between phonological and orthographic processing than children who spell well. Because they cannot conjure up a word image from the orthographic processor, they remain overly dependent on sound. Print provides children with a "schema for conceptualizing and analyzing the structure of speech" (Ehri 1984, p. 145).

Ehri (1986) also points out that in the general population, reading and spelling knowledge are highly correlated with one another, and average people can usually spell words they have read several times. Reading words in context, however, is not as instructive for spelling as reading them in isolation, because complete processing of all the word's features is not necessary for reading. In Ehri's view, connectionism and dual-route theory should be criticized for emphasizing the separateness of linguistic codes rather than their interdependence. However, Ehri's work has not focused on individuals with learning disabilities or adults with neurological damage, and does not account for the special cases of individuals with selective damage to one type of linguistic code.

Phoenician and Chinese: What About Individual Differences of "Modality Preference" in Normal Adults?

The mental processes employed by adults who have not suffered any overt or measurable neurological damage may be somewhat variable from one individual to another. Individual variation in component spelling skills appears to characterize mature adults who spell within the average range. Some show superiority in phonetic representation, or good ability to spell nonsense words phonetically, and accurate spelling by sound-symbol matching, but others seem to rely more on direct recall of established visual-orthographic memories and are not particularly adept at phonological analysis or phonetic representation. Most adults are satisfactory at both phonetic spelling and direct recall of whole words, but because each of these underlying subskills is normally distributed, there may be specialists at each end of those somewhat separate distributions. According to this theory of subskill distribution, some people would be relatively adept at phonetic spelling strategies, while others would be relatively adept at visual-orthographic memorization, particularly those with limited hearing. Stanovich (1988) represented possible patterns of variation in terms of reading behavior, but a similar model may apply to spelling as well.

While most people fall in the middle of a continuum of spelling "styles," the extreme examples of these subtypes were once dubbed "Phoenician" and "Chinese" (Baron and Strawson 1976; Treiman 1984; Treiman and Baron 1983). Phoenicians were said to rely heavily on spelling-sound rules. They were good at spelling nonsense words and good at generating plausible phonetic equivalents for unknown words. They were relatively less good at recalling exception words. "Chinese," on the other hand, relied more on word-specific associations from the graphemic processor. They were less good at spelling nonsense words by rule and generated errors that are more orthographically similar to the target word than phonetically similar. These contrasting styles were found in normal adults as well as in normal children (Treiman and Baron 1983), and were not necessarily associated with spelling disability. "Phoenicians" tended to be better readers than "Chinese," however (Baron and Treiman 1980). Stanovich (1992) emphasized that "Chinese" are characterized by the *lack* of an important linguistic skill (phonemic coding) as well as by their compensatory strategy of whole word memorization.

Given the preponderance of evidence that phonemic coding skills are extremely important in proficient spelling, these "modality" or "learning style" differences may simply reflect different levels of spelling skill and/or the effects of instruction (Gough and Walsh 1991) within the broad range of individual differences accepted as "normal." Instructional method, and the specific emphasis on phonemic analysis and sound-symbol relationships that a student has experienced, does influence the extent to which subjects will spell with good phonetic equivalents (Treiman and Baron 1983). Children and adults who demonstrate the "Chinese" strategy may well have at least subtle deficits in phonological processing ability or a "tin ear" for language. More will be said on this topic in Chapter 4, in the discussion of spelling disability.

Handwriting and Spelling

Our memories for letter sequences are not stored soley as kinesthetic or motor memories, because spelling can be generated in other modalities—through typing, movement of letter tiles, multiple choice selection, and oral spelling. Nevertheless, when we write or type, motor sequences seem to be automatic or preprogrammed for learned words. We execute them without conscious thought. Certainly, when children or adults have difficulty with letter formation or handwriting, their spelling is often impaired as well. What role, then, does handwriting play in spelling production?

In the time necessary to produce a written word, hand movements are programmed at a later processing stage than the mental retrieval of the spelling image from long-term memory. After a word is retrieved from memory, the letter string is held temporarily in a short-term memory store (the "graphemic buffer"). Then the mode of expression is selected and output is organized and executed. Cases have been reported of "specific agraphia," the impairment of the written generation of words, with preservation of the ability to type and spell orally (Goodman and Caramazza 1986). Thus an individual's output channel that converts the graphemic code to letter shapes, letter sequences, and motor patterns may be selectively impaired, but may leave the person able to spell by other means. When slips of the pen occur, a person's stored image of a word may be correct, but "blips" in the sequential production of letters may result in substitutions, omissions, additions, and order errors. "Blips" often involve omission of letters that recur in a word or sequence, suggesting that the placekeeping function of the motor production system is malfunctioning.

Although the relationship between handwriting and spelling has not been researched in any depth, manual writing does seem to reinforce the habit for a learned word. Fernald (1943) based an entire approach to reading and spelling on tracing and writing whole words to form habits. When children write a word the wrong way repeatedly, before learning it correctly, the incorrect word habit can be hard to break and the correct habit can be difficult to establish.

Dissection of the processing components of spelling in adults still leaves many questions about the development of spelling in children and the steps by which the visual-orthographic memory store, the phonological processing system, and written word memories are established. Models of spelling processes in adults should be applied cautiously in explaining spelling behavior in children. Nevertheless, the general architecture of the language processors and the unique functions they serve are certainly helpful in constructing a conceptual map of spelling acquisition.

RECOMMENDED READING

Ellis, A.W. 1993. *Reading, Writing, and Dyslexia: A Cognitive Analysis*, 2nd Edition. Hove, UK: Lawrence Erlbaum.

This concise, understandable book explains how cognitive neuropsychologists use behavioral studies to map brain function, construct theories of the psychological processes involved in reading and writing, and explain individual differences in reading and spelling ability.

Sterling, C.M., and Robson, C. 1992. *Psychology, Spelling, and Education*. Clevedon, United Kingdom: Multilingual Matters.

The collection of papers in this book were written by cognitive neuropsychologists, educators, and linguists of the British school. The interested reader would find this an excellent introduction to dual route theory and its implications.

CHAPTER 3

Spelling Development

According to numerous studies conducted over the past twenty years, spelling development occurs in a broadly predictable sequence. Researchers have documented similarities in the ways children learn to spell in spite of differences in their educational and family backgrounds and the rate at which they learn. The "stages" they go through have been described in several ways. Charles Read (1971, 1986) and Carol Chomsky (1979) were first to explain how preschool children's early spellings evolve from their developing awareness of phonology as well as their knowledge of the alphabet. In the decade following Chomsky's and Read's innovative interpretations of preschool children's creative spellings, other faculty and graduate students at Harvard applied and extended their ideas, generating both a theory of spelling development and insights into spelling disability (e.g., Bissex 1980; Chomsky 1971, 1979; Cook 1981; Moats 1983; Paul 1976). Simultaneously, at the University of Virginia, Professor Edmund Henderson, along with his graduate students and colleagues, produced a series of studies on elementary school children's spelling strategies and their acquisition of word knowledge (e.g., Beers 1980; Beers and Henderson 1977; Gentry 1978; Schlagal 1982). The Virginia researchers have validated their model of spelling acquisition and shown how stage of spelling development influences response to instruction (Henderson 1990; Invernizzi, Abouzeid, and Gill 1994; Morris, Nelson, and Perney 1986; Templeton and Bear 1992; Zutell 1992). Most recently, Treiman (1993) has shown through detailed analysis of first graders' spellings the ways in which phonological and visual-orthographic processing interact in learning to spell. I am indebted to all of the above for information contained in the following discussion.

Learning the letters in words is not analogous to stringing beads in visual memory. Neither reading nor spelling ability develops in a linear, additive fashion. Rather, the connections children make between sounds and symbols are mediated by implicit and explicit concepts about words that change as new information is assimilated (Ehri 1986, 1994; Gill 1992; Henderson 1990). Memories for specific words are influenced by the learner's perception of the speech sounds that compose them and the learner's knowledge of orthography. The acquisition of this knowledge occurs in a more or less predictable sequence throughout the elementary years. At each developmental stage, some conventions of orthography are mastered to an automatic level, while new ones are being assimilated. As new writing vocabulary is acquired, new orthographic patterns are attended to, extracted and recognized as units, and remembered in relation to what is already known. Moreover, learning to spell entails revision of previous concepts about words. Like other domains of cognitive and language development, spelling depends upon pattern extraction, differentiation of elements, and generalization of patterns through successive approximations of "correct" responses.

Several cautions are in order regarding the following blueprint of spelling development. First, children's rate of progress through the sequence of development varies enormously, with some children never accomplishing the more advanced levels. Also, as Ehri (1992) has commented, the notion of plateaus or stages may be neither accurate nor necessary in describing spelling development. Spelling development involves the continuous acquisition of various kinds of orthographic knowledge. In any child's writing, evidence of several "stages" may be present, although one type of error may predominate. Further, the order in which patterns are learned will be influenced by instruction (Tangel and Blachman 1995). For example, in Tangel and Blachman's study, children who had received explicit practice with short vowel encoding spelled consonant-vowel-consonant patterns more accurately than children who had not received explicit practice. Finally, a student's level of spelling development is most accurately detected in his or her misspellings of words at his or her instructional level (Morris 1992; Morris et al. in press). If words are too difficult or unfamiliar, the typical features of a developmental level may not be evident because the writer may resort to regressed or random attempts.

STAGES OF SPELLING DEVELOPMENT[1]
Early Stages of Spelling Development

Precommunicative writing. Most young children who are exposed to print in their homes will begin to experiment with writing spontaneously.

---

[1]The following description of spelling stages is partial to theory and research that has emphasized the link between speech processing and writing (Ehri 1987, 1989; Gentry 1981; Hoffman and Norris 1989; Read 1986; Treiman 1993). It is less influenced by theory concerned with orthographic knowledge per se (Henderson 1990; Schlagal 1992; Templeton and Bear 1992). Henderson and his colleagues focused on the emergence and consolidation of visual-orthographic knowledge in children's spelling and labeled the stages as follows:

Their writing has been referred to as "deviant spelling" by Gentry (1981) and as "garble" by others. Although, at this preliterate stage, children may know the names of some letters and be able to recognize letter forms, they do not know the alphabetic principle, or the idea that letters represent speech sounds. They also may not know the concept of wordness, or the idea that print represents words and spaces represent the boundaries between them. They often believe that phrases such as "over there" or "time to go to bed" or "thank you" are all one unit of expression. At this phase, however, their attempts to imitate adult writing may include letter forms, letter-like forms, number-like forms, and idiosyncratic symbols (figure 3).

Figure 3. "Come to the party at 1:00." Precommunicative writing at age 4.

Writing may go from left to right but often goes up, down, and back-wards. After a message is "written" the child can assign a meaning to it and read it back, but as time elapses, that meaning may be forgotten or changed. Reading at this stage is "logographic" or a process of guessing at whole words based on their visual features (Frith and Frith 1983).

Semiphonetic stage. After many experiments with imitative writing have occurred, and the child has developed awareness of alphabet letter names, a shift occurs in which the child realizes that letters represent speech sounds (Bissex 1980; Gentry 1981; Henderson 1990). This point of insight usually results in abbreviated or economical spellings wherein a few letters, usually consonants, are used selectively and rulefully to represent words and syllables. At this stage, the letters are usually strung together with little or no awareness of word boundaries. Letters are likely to be used for salient con-sonant sounds in particular, most often the initial consonants or pieces of words that are easily matched with an alphabet letter name. At this stage, children may also be reading according to partial phonetic cues (Ehri 1994),

---

Prephonetic, Letter Name, Within Word Pattern, Syllable Juncture, and Derivational constancy. Ehri (1986:1994), who extended and refined Frith's (1980) earlier concepts of logographic, alphabetic, and ortho-graphic stages of learning, proposes that the beginning stages of reading and spelling development be called **Precommunicative, Semiphonetic, Phonetic, and Morphemic.** The conception of development offered in this book is a composite of these perspectives with levels entitled **Precommunicative, Semiphonetic, Phonetic, Transitional, and Morphophonemic.**

most of which are also derived from their knowledge of letter names. Their spelling attempts will often show undifferentiated and unrefined ability to identify the phonemes in words, although they are employing the alphabetic principle as they use letters to represent speech sounds. Glenda Bissex (1980) reported these examples from her five-year-old son: RUDF (Are you deaf?) and HAPEBRTDA (Happy Birthday). Others, from a precocious four-year old, are shown in figure 4.

Figure 4. Phonetic spellings of a precocious 4 year old.

Phonetic spelling. As children gain more experience with print, and are encouraged to write, they learn consistently to represent all of the phonemes in words using strategies derived from their knowledge of letter names and some sound-letter correspondences. The spelling process, as described by Chomsky (1979), Read (1986), and Treiman (1993), is creative and driven by attention to articulatory phonetic detail. Although Read's first subjects were 32 precocious four- and five-year olds whose parents were graduate students, his discovery that children devised similar strategies and made similar phonological judgments about words entirely independently of one another was remarkable and innovative at that time. Subsequently, the predominant characteristics of his subjects' inventive spelling were documented in less gifted and somewhat older children as well (Beers 1980; Paul 1976; Treiman 1993).

At the phonetic spelling stage, children have at their command a repertoire of letter names and some learned sound-letter associations by which they represent all speech sounds in words systematically. The spelling representations are of surface phonetic features, not underlying phonemic or morphemic word structures. The child's phonetic analyses rely heavily on sound segmentation and articulatory-phonetic feedback, so much so that one could term this stage "spelling by mouth" rather than "spelling by sound."

Vowel spellings. At the phonetic spelling level, children represent long or tense vowels with reference to the letter name most like the tense vowel. They have not learned the convention that in English, many tense vowels are represented with combinations of vowel letters, and they spell with one letter for one sound, as follows:

DA (day) KAM (came) FEL (feel) LIK (lik) KUT (cute) BOT (boat)

Children also rely on their knowledge of alphabet letter names to derive many of their early phonetic spellings of short or lax vowels. Letter names are used creatively when lax vowels are paired with letter names articulated in similar position. This phenomenon of articulatory association might best be understood with reference back to the "vowel valley" diagram in Chapter 1 (figure 1). The most common principles of representation are as follows:

Short *i* [I] is derived from the letter name *E* : FES (fish); WEL (will).

Short *e* [ɛ] is derived from the letter name *A*: BAD (bed); SAD (said).

Short ā [æ] is derived from the letter name *A*: DAD (dad)

Short *u* [ʌ] is derived from the letter name *I*: KIT (cut); MIH (much)

Short *o* [ɑ] is derived from the letter name *I*: GIT (got); CLIK (clock)

Short u as in *put* is derived from the letter name *O*: SOGH (sugar), WOD (wood)

Back, rounded vowels are often represented with the lips rounded in /w/ position, for example in SOWN (soon), GOWT (goat), and POWLEOW (polio). Diphthongs are often represented in a phonetically literal manner as well, with both parts of the segmented vowel shown with separate letters: BOE (boy), HAUS (house), PIYL (pile).

Consonant spellings. Not all consonant phonemes in English are directly represented by alphabet letters in the orthography, so some must be derived creatively by beginning spellers, again by reference to articulation of letter names. The affricates [č] and [š] are often derived from letter name H, since it is the only letter name with an affricate. Thus, spellings such as WOH (watch), HRH (church), and WEH (witch) are sometimes produced, although the [š] is more likely to be classified with the fricative [s], as in SOW (show). The glide [j] which begins the word yellow is not in the letter name *Y*, so at times is paired with the letter name *U*, as in ULO (yellow). Likewise, the letter name *Y* contains the speech sound [w], and is used to write words such as YOH (watch), YL (will), and YAR (where).

Can children reread their phonetic spellings? Gill (1992) demonstrated that children could reread their invented spellings as well as they could read standard spellings. He speculated that "spelling and word recognition actually draw on the same orthographic knowledge base and the features children represent in their invented spellings are largely the same features they use to recognize or read standard spellings" (p. 92).

As children progress with their ability to represent speech sounds at a surface phonetic level, they are continuously being exposed to print and increasing their reading vocabulary. Most students spontaneously notice and mentally categorize redundant orthographic patterns in the words they are learning to read, but do so most quickly when orthographic sequences are pointed out to them through categorization, word search, and word analysis activities (Adams 1990). Their spelling increasingly incorporates information they have learned about the phonic elements of consonants, vowels, consonant blends, and consonant digraphs. However, the principle of successive approximations applies to this type of learning as well as to others; it is not uncommon for children to "invent" digraphs or overgeneralize them, for example, or to begin placing a "silent e" at the end of most words. As children's knowledge of words is informed by the specifics of sound-symbol correspondence, some associations become automatic, and larger orthographic patterns become the focus of learning. According to connectionist theory, the association weights between the most common sounds and symbols are strengthened to the point of automatic, accurate retrieval. The surface level, sound-by-sound strategy of the phonetic stage yields to more complex, abstract, and multilevel concepts about print and its relationship with speech. Children usually give up their belief that one letter spells one sound during first grade, and are working with more complex ideas about graphemes by the end of first grade to the middle of second grade. For example, one first-grade girl's spellings of frequently written words[2] changed as follows over a period of several months:

AKT	ASKT	ASKED		
NET	NAET	NEAT		
SLLE	SALLE	SALEE	SILLEY	SILLY
TGK	THIEK	TANGK	THINGK	THIGK
FLLAOWZ	FLLAWRZ	FLAWRS	FLOWERS	
HAOS	HOOS	HOES	HOSE	HOUSE

Transitional Spelling: Within-Word Patterns and Beyond

After children gain more experience with print and increase their silent reading ability, they realize that the speech-spelling correspondence system is governed by many of the constraints reviewed in Chapter I and that graphemes are most often groups of letters. They recognize that silent letters can occur in graphemes and that tense vowel spellings are most often composed of two or more vowel letters. They usually include a vowel in a syllable, although the vowel may be misplaced. They experiment with doubled letters and begin to internalize common syllable patterns. Consider, for example, the spellings of H.H., a bright boy with delayed spelling development entering fourth grade:

BECK (back)	PAPRES (papers)
COL (call)	MOVEING (moving)
BOWN (down)	PLAITID (planted)
HIAR (hair)	SRATE (straight)
NHITE (night)	MIINIT (minute)
BOKING (broken)	

These spellings, at face value, are not as phonetically accurate as spellings typical of the earlier phonetic spelling stage. Is this student more or less advanced? In order to progress, the developing speller must abandon the surface phonetic, linear approach to representing each sound segment. This student is progressing conceptually as he learns more words; he understands that many graphemes are more than one letter and he is spelling tense vowels

[2]Data from case study on "Sarah," by Susan Sowers, University of New Hampshire, 1978.

in a way that follows orthographic, rather than purely letter name/phonetic principles. He uses two letters to spell tense vowels, not just a single letter name. He doubles the letter *i*, again showing knowledge of the occurrence of doubling without knowing the specific instances in which it is allowed. He puts a vowel letter *e* after the syllabic /r/ in PAPRES, apparently realizing that syllables need vowel letters in English and *e* can serve as a marker. (A less mature spelling of this word might be PAPRS). This boy's subtle problems with phonological processing do surface in his omission of consonants in the clusters /str/ and /br/ and confusion of the phonetically similar endings "ing" and "en," but he is in transition to mature spelling.

Early transitional spellings may appear to be bizarre or off-base because developing concepts about print are often applied in the wrong instance or with the wrong combination of letters. Are any of the following spellings for *night*—NIT, NITE, or NHITE—better or worse than the others in terms of either phonetic accuracy or orthographic accuracy? The first is certainly phonetically accurate, by early phonetic stage principles. The last, although the letter order is inaccurate, is a more advanced approximation of the word than the other two, because it reflects partial orthographic memory. The spelling suggests readiness for direct instruction in the "ight" pattern, whereas the child who spells the more immature NIT might not be ready to assimilate that information.

Morphophonemic Spelling: The Integration of Meaning, Sound, and Orthographic Patterns

Inflections.   After learning the graphemes that represent consonant and vowel spellings within a syllable, children must then learn to recognize common ways in which meaning influences spelling in combination with sound-symbol correspondence. Inflections, the meaningful grammatical endings that do not change the part of speech of a word to which they are added, provide the first introduction to the relationship between meaning and spelling. Inflected endings, the past tense *-ed,* the plural *-s,* the *-ing* morpheme, the comparatives *-er* and *-est,* and the agentive *-er,* are usually part of first and second graders' oral language competence. These endings occur very frequently in the texts that young children read and write, and thus exposure to these forms and opportunities to spell them are present early on. Most average children abstract these patterns and implicitly recognize their status as linguistic units in first and second grade (Rubin 1988; Rubin, Patterson, and Kantor 1991). Children who are progressing normally internalize the fixed spellings of inflections between second- and third-grade level (Bailet 1990; Beers and Beers 1992; Schwartz and Doehring 1977).

Some inflection spellings do not follow sound-symbol correspondence principles because they retain consistent spellings even when they change in pronunciation. At earlier stages of development, children will spell these endings phonetically. In the case of the past tense, which is spoken phonetically in three different forms as /d/, /t/, and /əd/, children will produce forms such as WAKT (walked), PED or PIND (pinned), and WOTID (wanted). In order to progress beyond phonetically accurate production, children must integrate meaning, sound, and symbol, and realize that when certain meaningful units are involved, the spelling stays consistent and even takes precedence over sound. For example, in order to spell the word *talked,* the child must realize that the word has two meaningful parts, *talk* and *ed,* both of which are spelling units, but that it has only one spoken syllable. The morpheme [əd] does not have syllable status; it is reduced to one unvoiced and unaspirated stop [t] in certain words. Yet it must be apprehended as a spelling unit that remains consistent in spite of three phonetic transformations. Further, the child has to discriminate these endings from other word-final instances of [t] that are not morphemic, such as in *last* and *kept.*

A similar problem exists with the phonetic segment [ər]. Sometimes it corresponds to a morpheme, as in *maker* (agentive) and *higher* (comparative), and sometimes it has no morpheme status as in *number* and *silver.* First, children must learn that as a syllable, the morphene -er requires a vowel letter and cannot be spelled with syllabic letter *r.* Children must learn eventually that when -er is added to a root, some orthographic change rules might apply to the base word if it ends with an *e* or a *y* (*baker* and *prettier*). They will also have to learn that agentive [ər] can be spelled -er and -or; the first spelling is more common, and the second occurs most often with words of Latin origin (*conductor, inspector*).

Homophones and compounds. At the transition from phonetic to morphemic spelling, children also must begin to differentiate homophones and compounds. Words such as *two, to,* and *too,* or *aloud* and *allowed* sound the same but can be spelled correctly only if one knows their meaning. As Henderson (1990) emphasizes, these forms are more than "demons"; they can be learned in meaningful phrases and should be used to represent an important principle of English spelling. Compounds, also, must be recognized as such. Words such as *playmate, something,* and *boyfriend,* are more likely to be spelled correctly if the compound structure, with the stress on the first word, is recognized. For example, the *oy* in *boyfriend* would be an *oi* if the word were not a compound.

Early derivational morphemes. Basic prefixes and suffixes are also learned at this stage, particularly the forms that do not require a phonological or orthographic transformation of the root or base word to which the affix is attached (*un-, re-, dis-; -ment, -ness, -ful*). By fourth grade, most average students are generalizing their knowledge of prefixes, suffixes, and roots to decipher the meanings of hundreds of new words encountered in reading (Myerson 1978; Tyler and Nagy 1987; Wysocki and Jenkins 1987). Before that point, children must have developed at least a rudimentary awareness of these common affixes as their speaking vocabulary expands. To spell words with prefixes and suffixes, children must become aware of the phenomenon of schwa or the unaccented vowel [ə]. In multisyllable words with affixes, especially those of Latin origin, the accent or stress is usually on the root morpheme; the affixes are often spoken with a reduced vowel whose identity cannot be determined from pronunciation alone (*television, incomparable, benefactor*). Knowing the meaning of the affix and its standard spelling, however, can resolve the ambiguity created by the reduction of the spoken vowel. For example, the "pre" in *prescription,* or the *"re"* in *reduce* are difficult to identify if one relies only on speech because they are unaccented. They should be learned as meaningful prefixes with standard spellings.

Stage of Spelling Development and Spelling Achievement

The developmental characteristics of a child's spellings corresponds to his or her level of spelling achievement. The more advanced the quality of a child's misspellings, the more advanced his or her storehouse of spelling knowledge is likely to be. Bear (1992) has shown that spelling achievement level in first through third graders, as measured by number of words correct on a standardized spelling test, corresponded well to the characteristics of their spelling errors. Close correspondence would be expected, as knowledge of how the spelling system represents sound mediates what children remember about words (Ehri and Robbins 1992). Children at the same age and grade level, however, may differ considerably in their stage of development, as illustrated by the following three second graders, who differed over a range of about six months on an achievement test (table 7):

The first child is not yet able to produce phonetic spellings reliably; the second child is an accurate phonetic speller; and the third child is "transitional" in that he or she knows many more orthographic rules and conventions than the other two. Child #1 may need to focus on speech sound awareness and basic consonant and vowel correspondences in one-syllable words; Child #2 may be ready for the more complex and conditional vowel and consonant correspondences; and Child #3 seems ready to study words with more than one syllable. Instruction can, and should, be matched to the level of knowledge the child is ready to assimilate.

TABLE 7   EXAMPLES OF SECOND GRADERS' SPELLINGS

Given Word	Child #1	Child #2	Child #3
written	wiger	ritn	writen
captain	cuper	capdn	captin
loose	lise	lus	loos
struck	stser	srek	struck
fullest	fulles	flisd	fullist
wear	waer	yare	were
cared	cudsed	kard	carde
knew	new	new	new
easy	eses	eze	esey
load	lede	lod	lode
lesson	lise	lasn	lessen
use	urst	yus	yoos
began	begon	began	beagan
dresser	tress	drsr	dreser
glass	gress	glas	glass
trouble	trub	trubl	truble
helicopter	heltiea	hlacap	hellacopter
Yankee-Doodle	yenoonm	ykedudl	yankeydoodle

Spelling Development is Influenced by Instruction

One of the most common misinterpretations of the literature on spelling development is that children should be left to come by their spelling skill naturally, in the course of experimentation with writing, and that direct instruction in spelling is unnecessary. While it is true that what children learn is mediated by their concepts of phonology and their knowledge of the writing system, and a few children appear to teach themselves how to spell, the majority learn faster if they are taught directly.

Recent studies by Griffith (1991), Tangel and Blachman (1992; 1995), and Uhry and Shepherd (1993) have shown that children progress faster in spelling and reading if they are taught how to analyze speech sounds in words and taught how to spell them by using sound-symbol correspondence. Tangel and Blachman (1995), working with low-income, inner-city children in public schools, demonstrated that children who were taught in kindergarten and first grade to be aware of phonemes in words and taught to connect those sounds with specific spellings did better than comparison children on several measures. Children who were taught directly were more advanced in the quality of their misspellings, knew more words on a standardized spelling test, and were able to decode unfamiliar words more accurately than children who had been taught with basal readers but who had not had the explicit training in sound-symbol correspondence. Uhry and Shepherd's (1993) study was similar; instruction in segmenting and counting the phonemes in words and subsequent practice representing them with letters led to advantages for first-grade children in a whole language classroom. The children who received direct practice in segmenting and spelling words did better at nonsense-word reading, real-word reading, sound segmentation, and spelling. Although the children were in classrooms that encouraged creative spelling during writing, those who were taught more deliberately, with emphasis on sequential sound-symbol matching, learned faster. The children in Tangel and Blachman's first-grade group, after explicit training, were able to spell constructions such as "ed" and consonant blends better than the group studied by Treiman (1993), who were in a program emphasizing informal and incidental exposure to spelling patterns.

DEVELOPMENT OF INTERMEDIATE AND ADVANCED SPELLING

Whether formal spelling instruction is given or not, middle-grade and high-school students usually continue to develop their spelling skills. Although we know less about the nature and sequence of later stages of spelling development than we do about development prior to fifth grade, we do know that children continue to develop their concepts of orthography and their ability to associate spelling patterns with speech patterns in the middle grades. As children learn more words, and have more examples in memory of redundant spelling patterns, they can rely increasingly on analogy strategies to spell (Ehri 1987, 1989; Goswami 1988; Marsh et al. 1980; Simon and Simon 1973). In addition, they become increasingly more aware of phonological shifts and the phonological relationships among words with morphological derivations (Carlisle 1987; Templeton 1992; Templeton and Scarborough-Franks 1985) and may employ this knowledge to generate a correct spelling when a word cannot be recalled visually. Finally, more capable spellers become able to use multiple sources of linguistic information about words—orthographic, phonological, and etymological—to facilitate spelling memory and recall, if and when necessary.

Spelling By Analogy

Even kindergarteners and first graders incorporate letter sequences and patterns that they learn in reading into their inventive spellings (Ehri and

Robbins 1992; Goswami and Bryant 1990; Treiman 1993). They must, because the transition to the use of correct graphemes, syllable patterns, and morphemes could not occur if beginning spellers relied exclusively on individual letter-sound correspondences, given the nature of the English correspondence system. Individual letter-sound analysis is necessary in order to build perception of and memory for larger subunits, such as onsets and rimes (Ehri and Robbins 1992; Treiman 1986), but these basic building blocks are organized into larger units in orthographic memory, especially when they are common or redundant. For example, the patterns *tion* and *able* are probably stored as units.

Spelling by analogy becomes increasingly important as children reach the middle grades and have mastered simpler sound-symbol correspondences and syllable patterns. Analogous reasoning in spelling as well as specific visual memory for words has been shown to account for the fact that normally progressing fourth graders could outspell a computer algorithm that relied only on sound-symbol correspondence rules to spell (Simon and Simon 1973). The knowledge of fifth graders includes specific letter sequences and spelling patterns within and across syllable boundaries that can be applied to spelling nonsense words like *zoldier* and *cuscular* (Marsh et al. 1980). Spelling by analogy can occur because information about words in visual-orthographic memory is organized according to many levels of linguistic structure. Phonetic, phonological, graphemic, morphological, and syntactic features are remembered as related facets of the same word concept (Adams 1990; Ehri 1989). These word features are cross-referenced in memory. When one aspect of a word image is activated in memory, the other known features are also activated along with other words that share those features. Accumulating this knowledge base is a protracted developmental process. Words are learned in stages and word concepts are elaborated gradually with experience. Knowledge may be incomplete and unelaborated, as it might be for the learner who encounters a word for the first time, or it may involve a deep, thorough, and explicit image of all aspects of a word's form and meaning, such as a linguist or dictionary author might hold.

The process by which pattern redundancies are extracted from words is to a great degree implicit or unintentional (Ehri 1987; Fischer, Shankweiler, and Liberman 1985; Goswami 1992; Schwartz and Doehring 1977; Templeton 1992) and the better one reads and spells the more easily the implicit feature extraction process seems to work. Competent spellers, even though they may not be able to explain why words are spelled the way they are, will spontaneously notice similarities between words in print. They then exploit this knowledge in their spelling. Normally progressing students also seem to employ a "linguistic monitoring device" (Simon 1976) that detects phonological and orthographic oddities and that facilitates self-correction of errors. This built-in proofreading capability operates better when it is applied to other people's writing than when it is applied to one's own.

Awareness of Phonological Shifts

Phonological rule knowledge governing the production of word derivations such as *preside-president; succeed-succession* (Templeton 1992) develops at least through tenth grade in average students. Children as young as third grade begin systematically to apply knowledge of sound patterns in related words such as *sane-sanity, relate-relation,* and *human-humanity* in their oral language (Meyerson 1978). However, knowledge of complex derivational relationships and the phonological shifts that accompany them, as in words like *decide-decision, magic-magician,* seem to be greatly facilitated by exposure to print. Regular vowel alternation patterns in oral language, those involving vowel laxing (*sane-sanity*) and vowel reduction (*define-definition*), continue to be learned in high school (Carlisle 1987; Templeton and Scarborough-Franks 1985). The older the student, the more likely he or she is to generate correct word derivations orally and in writing, at least through tenth grade. Experience with print, rather than experience with oral language alone, seems to be critical in the development of this advanced level of morpho-phonological rule application (Templeton and Scarborough-Franks 1985). Written language contains far more examples of these derivational relationships than a person is likely to encounter in spoken language.

Templeton (1980) tested good spellers in grades six, eight, and ten, to see if a visual or auditory presentation of a base word would be more helpful in triggering a correct pronunciation of a derived word when the derivation involved a phonological change in the base word. Seeing base words, as opposed to hearing them, significantly increased the probability of students correctly pronouncing words such as *contrition, urbanity*, and *verbosity*. In addition, the correct pronunciation of the derived words with vowel shifts was facilitated when a sentence context for the word was provided. Most students could spell the nonsense words correctly, better than they could pronounce them, again suggesting that experience with print was more important than oral language exposure in learning the relationships between pronunciation and meaningful word relationships. Because spoken language obscures many derivational word relationships and written language preserves them (Chomsky 1970), as in *anxious* and *anxiety; wild* and *wilderness; equate* and *equanimity,* we may learn them more easily by reading and writing them than by hearing them. Most people become educated about language structure from experience with print.

Competent language learners spontaneously use derivational word relationships productively after seeing very few examples. Average students at about an eighth grade level, however, have been found to be unable to explain that orthography visually preserves meaning across related words such as *restore* and *restoration* (Templeton 1992). Further, Henderson (1990) and colleagues (Templeton and Bear 1992) have shown that students must have mastered principles of syllable juncture, such as when to double letters and when to drop an "e" before adding an ending, before they can engage in explicit morphological analysis. Advanced spelling ability depends on the integrity of learning at earlier developmental stages, those stages concerned with phoneme mapping, syllable patterns, and syllable connections.

Use of Multiple Sources of Linguistic Information

Derived words that have complex relationships with their roots, especially those that involve phonological shifts (*explore-exploration; precise-precision*) are harder for both normally progressing students and poor spellers to learn (Carlisle 1987; Fischer, Shankweiler, and Liberman 1985). Complex word structure is inherently more difficult for most people because the learner must layer one type of linguistic knowledge on another. The learner must be secure with sound-symbol correspondence, and then accommodate additional information about word derivation, pronunciation changes, and orthographic rules. Predictably, those who have difficulty memorizing spelling vocabulary seem to lack the linguistic sensitivity to attend to and remember several layers of language structure. The ability to notice word structure at the sound, syllable, and morpheme levels simultaneously is associated with better memory for learned words.

SUMMARY

Children do follow a predictable sequence in learning to spell, whether they learn slowly or quickly. To begin to spell, a child must have a sense of the internal structure of words. Phonetic spelling is a necessary step in early spelling development that signifies readiness for formal spelling instruction. Children who have become aware enough of word structure to spell phonetically can then learn the more complex graphemes that make up most spellings for sounds. Those who can identify, sequence, and segment speech sounds and who are taught to make letter-sound matches learn to spell more rapidly than children who simply invent spelling when the need arises in their writing activities. Those children also make more rapid progress in reading.

Orthographic knowledge is acquired in a roughly predictable sequence, from individual letters, to patterns within words, to patterns that exist across several syllables. As the patterns of orthography are learned, the influence of meaning on spelling can also be assimilated; the spellings for morphemes including prefixes, roots, suffixes, and grammatical endings can be learned as stable forms. Good spellers are those who have learned to attend to several levels of word structure—sounds, syllables, and meaningful parts, as well as orthographic conventions for representing them. Learning to spell is both conceptual and associative; children must learn the principles of written language representation and remember specific words.

RECOMMENDED READING

Read, C. 1986. *Children's Creative Spelling.* Boston: Routledge and Kegan Paul.

Read's lucid work explains the phonological underpinnings of children's early spellings from a linguistic perspective.

Templeton, S., and Bear, D. B. 1992. *Development of Orthographic Knowledge and the Foundations of Literacy: A Memorial Festschrift for Edmund Henderson.* Hillsdale, NJ: Lawrence Erlbaum Associates.

A book for the more seriously interested reader, it is a valuable compilation of the work of University of Virginia researchers.

Treiman, R.T. 1993. *Beginning to Spell.* New York: Oxford University Press.

A very detailed, meticulous analysis of the spellings first graders generated throughout their year in school. Through informed spelling error analysis, this book contributes evidence for the close relationship between spoken and written language processes in younger children.

CHAPTER 4

Spelling Errors and Spelling Disabilities

SPELLING DISABILITY IS A LINGUISTIC PROBLEM

Spelling difficulties are common among individuals with learning disabilities and are associated with most types of language and reading disorders. Poor spelling always exists with intrinsic reading disability (dyslexia) and may or may not be associated with mathematics calculation deficits. Specific spelling difficulty affects many individuals who have no other obvious learning disabilities (Frith 1980b), although subtle associated problems with language processing, such as learning a foreign language, are common in those individuals. For many literate people, spelling is a challenge, if not a source of consternation; the average adult with a high school education spells at the eighth grade level according the Wide Range Achievement Test normative tables (Jastak and Wilkinson 1984). Individuals with language-related learning disabilities make much less progress with spelling than reading, even with the advantages of an appropriate education, high IQ, and high socioeconomic status (Bruck 1987; Finucci, Gottfredson, and Childs 1985; Frauenheim and Heckerl 1983; Moats in press).

Contrary to logic, the written language skill (spelling) that is most evident in language-related learning disorders has received comparatively little attention in research. Some of our most well-funded studies of learning disabilities include no measures of spelling and no analysis of the relationship between reading and spelling. One might predict that a basic language function that presents such a challenge for so many would merit more attention because of its potential to shed light on the nature of specific language disability. However, spelling error analysis and spelling assessment are more difficult than they might appear on the surface, and complexity of measurement and interpretation may have discouraged many investigators.

Far from being a "mechanical" skill, as it is often characterized in writing tests (Hammill and Larson 1987), spelling is a multifaceted form of lin-

49

guistic representation that integrates and depends on phonological, morphological, semantic, and orthographic knowledge (Fischer, Shankweiler, and Liberman 1985; Henderson 1990; Hodges 1981; Read 1986; Frith 1980a). We know that in general, good spellers are more sensitive to language structure, more able to think about language and manipulate language, and more able to learn linguistic complexities than individuals who spell poorly (Bailet 1990; Bailet and Lyon 1985; Carlisle 1987; Liberman et al. 1985; Rubin, Patterson, and Cantor 1991). Conversely, those who spell poorly, even if they read well, usually demonstrate at least subtle difficulties with the manipulation of language, use of language, or the ability to notice language structure while remembering words. Thus for some children, learning to spell is natural in that they are neurologically well equipped to learn through exposure to written language. For others, learning to spell requires systematic, structured practice over a long period and nets only modest success.

Spelling competence has been shown many times over to have almost no relationship to non-symbolic, visual-spatial learning ability (Liberman et al. 1985; Sweeney and Rourke 1985; Vellutino 1979). This fact has been demonstrated again in the restandardization of the Wechsler Intelligence Scale for Children, Third Edition (Wechsler 1991). The correlation between the Perceptual Organization factor of the WISC-III and scores on the spelling test of the Wide Range Achievement Test (Jastak and Wilkinson 1984) is a very weak .09. Skills such as assembling puzzles, constructing block designs, and finding details in pictures do not predict spelling ability. As was described in Chapter 2, the visual component of spelling is closely linked to other linguistic functions and involves a special memory system that is used to store and recall images of print.

Within this general framework, several questions about spelling disability merit discussion. What does spelling error analysis contribute to understanding the nature of spelling disability? What is the relative contribution of phonological and visual-orthographic processing weaknesses to spelling disorders? Do individuals with spelling disabilities learn to spell differently, or are the stages of development similar in good and poor spellers? How are individuals with spelling disabilities different from one another?

ERROR ANALYSIS AND ITS CONTRIBUTION TO DIAGNOSIS
The Errors of Normally Developing Children

Not all phonological features and spelling patterns in words are equally easy for average children to learn. Before we can define and identify what constitutes a disability, we must take into account the intrinsic difficulties of certain aspects of written language and the fact that these are learned quite slowly, even by individuals without disabilities. It is known, for example, that at all stages of development, vowel spellings are more difficult and produce more errors than consonant spellings (Pennington et al. 1986; Schlagal 1992). Short vowels are difficult for children to discriminate auditorily and associate with symbols (Ehri, Wilce, and Taylor 1987); long vowels are difficult to remember orthographically, and vowel spellings are not mastered by most children until fourth grade (Schlagal 1992). Thus, it is expected that all children will make more errors on vowels and that vowel spellings will be challenging to teach.

According to Schlagal (1992), the consonants also vary in difficulty among each other. Preconsonantal nasals, such as the /m/ in *jump* and the /n/ in *went,* are more problematic than other consonants in the early stages of development. Consonant blends are much harder for normally progressing children than single consonants (Treiman 1993) and are mastered later. Omission of liquids (/l/, /r/) and nasals (/n/, /m/, /ŋ/) from consonant blends account for a significant proportion of errors through sixth grade (Hoffman and Norris 1989; Schlagal 1986, 1989; Sterling 1983). In all grades up to 6th and probably beyond, r-controlled vowels (*girl, turn*), consonant doubling (*pebble; sunny*) and recall of vowel markers (as in *gait* and *gate; feat* and *feet)* are relatively more difficult than other correspondences.

The ability to judge the sounds in words develops through progressive differentiation and refinement of phonological analysis (Read 1986). Children in the beginning stages of writing often use spellings for phonemes that share many features with the target phoneme, but are inexact in one or more features (Treiman 1993). For example, one fricative might be substituted for another, as in SE */she,* or one velar for another as in SIG /*sing.* As described in Chapter 3, children's judgments of vowels in certain contexts, such as before voiced velar consonants /g/ and /ŋ/, are literal and phonetically accurate; they spell exactly what they feel and/or hear until they become more abstract in their approach (Ehri et al. 1987; Read 1986). Thus, they might spell BAEG/bag, or PEG/pig, because the short vowels in these words are pronounced differently in anticipation of the velar consonants that follow them. In the first grade, vowel substitutions tend to be logical and made with vowels that are adjacent in articulation, particularly /E/ and /I/ (Ehri, Wilce, and Taylor 1987; Hoffman and Norris 1989). However, as they are exposed to written text, children's judgement of speech sounds is shaped and changed by their growing knowledge of spelling (Ehri 1989; Ehri and Wilce 1987).

Early spelling errors also mirror the normal phonological production errors characteristic of young children's speech (Hoffman and Norris 1989).

Before they achieve adult speech patterns, children's spoken language typically is marked by systematic simplification, deletion, and substitution of speech sounds ("goggie" for "doggy"; "so" for "sock"; "wawa" for "water," etc.). The same phonological principles that operate as children learn to speak seem to be reactivated and reemployed as they learn to spell. Children commonly omit consonants from clusters (CHAN/train), make errors on voiced/voiceless consonant pairs (NAJR/nature) or substitute front consonants for back ones (TIHN/kitchen) in their spelling, for example.

First-grade children learning to spell often treat some phoneme sequences as units within the syllable, especially the sequence of a vowel plus a nasal (JUP/jump) or a vowel plus a liquid (OD/old) (Treiman 1993). Such judgments show acute sensitivity to phonological reality: these phoneme sequences are coarticulated and the vowel-consonant identities are not distinct. These sounds form a "syllable peak" that is vocally one unit, according to Treiman. Because their boundaries are more imagined than real, the vowel-sonorant combinations are difficult to segment in spoken words and thus are frequently a source of spelling error.

Children learn gradually to identify and spell all phonemes in a word using standard graphemes, but only after many steps of successive approximation. As they learn to spell, they must also learn that phonetic variation in speech sound production, including aspiration, affrication, elongation, nasalization, and reduction of phonemes (see Chapter 1) is usually not represented in the spelling system.

Through grade six and beyond, a large proportion of common spelling errors occurs on words having suffixes that change the spelling of a base word, especially those that involve the doubling rule and the silent-e rule (Schlagal 1986, 1992; Sterling 1983). In one study of sixth-grade boys' spontaneous writing (Sterling 1983), a significant proportion of errors occurred on the nonsyllabic past tense (-ed pronounced as /t/ or /d/), and on ambiguous consonants such as /k/ which have several possible spellings. The spelling of unstressed schwa, /ə/, especially in longer words of Latin origin (Henry 1988), becomes an increasingly important source of error as children learn longer words in third grade and beyond. Schlagal (1992) reported that 62% of spelling errors at level V and 40% of spelling errors at Level VI on his Qualitative Inventory of Word Knowledge occurred on unstressed syllables. Other errors were attributable to lack of awareness of word origin and its relationship to spelling.

In summary, the error patterns in the misspellings of normal learners are driven by developmental factors, as discussed in the previous chapter, and are associated with (a) misinterpretation of phonological features of words (b) failure to differentiate or segment individual phonemes within the syllable (c) confusion of phonemes sharing articulatory features, such as back placement (d) failure to recognize the integrity of certain morphemes (e) failure to apply orthographic change rules, and (f) simple failure to remember which graphemes are used when speech sounds alone cannot be relied on *(ible* vs. *able)*.

If these linguistic variables determine what is easy and difficult for normally progressing children, then it is important to know whether children with specific language disabilities generate qualitatively different error patterns, and/or if they find specific words or linguistic features more difficult to spell than do normally progressing children. These insights, then, should help clarify the nature of spelling disability and what intervention approaches make sense.

The Error Patterns of Individuals with Spelling Disabilities

Over the past twenty years, some researchers have found diagnostically meaningful differences in the spelling error patterns of students with dyslexia (Boder 1973; Finucci et al. 1983; Snowling 1981), but others have not. Several recent studies have compared the spellings of older dyslexic students to those of normal younger children of similar spelling achievement level (Bruck and Waters 1988; Carlisle 1987; Moats 1983; Nelson 1980; Pennington et al. 1986; Worthy and Invernizzi 1990). Using structured spelling dictation tasks, these studies found rather uniformly that error patterns in older elementary students with poor spelling were similar to those of younger students who were matched on intelligence and achievement level. The errors of poor spellers were not found to be qualitatively distinctive or less phonetically accurate than those of younger students functioning at the same level of development. Other studies that have reported phonological errors in spelling-disabled students have often described students with global language disorders and low Verbal IQ, or students whose deficits were so great that they had not yet achieved phoneme awareness and the ability to spell phonetically.

The case study in table 8 illustrates the progression of a student with dyslexia through the normal stages of spelling development. This girl was tested five times between second and sixth grade with the Wide Range Achievement Test (Jastak and Wilkinson 1984). At the first testing, she was not able to spell phonetically. Some progress had been made by mid-third grade; some early phonetic strategies were used, but no more than three letters were employed for each word. By mid-fourth grade, after spelling instruction was initiated, this girl was able to spell phonetically at a preconventional level, and was achieving at beginning second-grade level. By sixth grade, her spelling improved significantly, although she regressed to preconventional strategies when presented with some unfamiliar words (PARCHS/ purchase). Her error pattern changed as she progressed, and the degree to which she would be described as "dysphonetic" in Boder's (1973) terminology would depend on the level at which she was tested. Other case studies are on record (Cook 1981) with similar findings.

TABLE 8 SPELLING DEVELOPMENT OF GIRL WITH READING AND SPELLING DISABILITY, IQ 95

	I	II	III	IV	V
Grade Placement	2.2	3.6	4.5	5.0	6.1
Age at Testing	7–2	8–6	9–4	10–0	11–1
*WRAT Reading	1.3	1.7	2.4	2.5	4.4
*WRAT Spelling	K.9	1.1	2.3	2.5	3.7

Given Word	*Child's Spellings at Each Testing*				
cat	CKD	cat	cat	cat	cat
in	les	in	in	in	in
boy	Bee	bog	boy	boy	boy
and	at	an	and	and	and
will	wh	we	will	will	will
make	pe	mac	mak	make	make
him	—	ham	ham	him	him
say	—	sat	sa	sais	say
cut	—	cut	cut	kut	cut
cook	—	cuc	cook	cook	cook
light		lut	lit	liet	light
must		mns	must	must	must
dress		drs	dras	dres	dress
reach		res	rech	rich	reach
order		rde	oridr	odroor	order
watch		wus	woch	woch	woch
enter		at	atr	entoor	enter
grown		got	gron	gron	grone
nature			nach	naech	nacher
explain			esplan	evispan	evsplan
edge			eth	eja	eny
kitchen			cachen	kichin	kichen
surprise					surprises
result					reseld
advice					parchs
brief					brefe

*Wide Range Achievement Test. Jastak and Wilkinson 1985.

Given the evidence that children with spelling disabilities progress through stages similar to those of students without disabilities, it might be logical to infer that spelling disability is simply a delay in acquisition of orthographic knowledge. One might expect that errors in very poor spellers would simply reflect a lower stage of spelling development, not an abnormal way of processing language. The characterization of spelling disability as a developmental delay in language acquisition may have merit, but it obviously leaves some critical questions unexplained. Teachers who work with individuals with spelling disabilities know that they experience word confusions, recall failures, and unexpected problems remembering certain words, and that they are not just like normally progressing students in the way they learn. In addition, longitudinal studies have shown clearly that those with specific language disabilities make very limited progress in spelling achievement up to adulthood. Children with reading and spelling disabilities, or even specific spelling disabilities alone, never master the more advanced stages of spelling (Bruck 1987). Typically, the gap between reading and spelling increases over time when remediation is successful with dyslexics. With good instruction, there may be an ever-widening gap between a student's increasing ability to write an organized composition and his or her lagging ability to spell. The question remains, why is spelling so difficult for some individuals? What insights might error patterns hold with regard to the nature of spelling disability?

Relationship between phoneme awareness and spelling. In order to learn to read and spell, children must be explicitly aware of the constituent phonemes in words (Ball 1993; Ehri and Robbins 1992; Goswami and Bryant 1990; Liberman, Shankweiler, and Liberman 1989; Tunmer and Hoover 1993; Treiman 1993). Evidence is substantial that specific reading disability is marked by deficits on phonemic awareness tasks and other skills dependent on phonemic processing (Felton and Wood 1989; Liberman and Shankweiler 1985; Lundberg 1994; Pennington et al. 1986; Rack, Snowling, and Olson 1992; Vellutino, Scanlon, and Tanzman 1994). Poor readers consistently have greater difficulty than good readers on tests of phoneme awareness (how many speech sounds are in toast?), phoneme segmentation (can you say meat without the /m/?), rhyming (what rhymes with stone?), fluency and accuracy of spoken word production, and nonsense word reading tasks. Poor spellers, both children and adults, also do poorly on tests of phonological processing (Foorman and Francis 1994; Goswami and Bryant 1990; Liberman et al. 1985; Lindamood 1993; Rohl and Tunmer 1988; Tangel and Blachman 1992). As with reading, when children are taught explicitly to identify the speech sounds in words, using exercises such as tracking sounds with colored blocks, their spelling improves (Bradley and Bryant 1983; Tangel and Blachman 1992, 1995). Especially in the beginning stages, spelling develops in accordance with one's ability to analyze the phonemes in words explicitly. When children can spell phonetically, they are ready to learn standard spellings. Phonological skill is most important for early spelling development, although memory for visual letter sequences is ultimately necessary for spelling proficiency.

As stated above, when older dyslexic children are compared to younger normal ones, many studies have found a similar proportion of phonetically accurate errors (Bailet 1990; Moats 1983; Nelson 1980; Worthy and Invernizzi 1990). These studies compared children on dictated word lists, and equated the good and poor spellers on general intelligence. Thus, the children with spelling disabilities did not have the type of global language disorder that would have lowered their verbal IQ scores, but were of average intelligence. In older poor spellers and younger normal children, errors are about 60 to 70% phonetically accurate on the whole, once children have reached the phonetic spelling stage. If children with spelling disability have phonological processing deficits, why are their errors not showing a higher rate of phonological misperception? Possibilities include design flaws in those studies, invalid methods of error analysis that are insensitive to real differences in phonological skill, or the chance that the phonological deficit hypothesis is inaccurate.

Morphophonemic awareness and spelling disability. Several researchers have found a higher incidence of errors involving inflected morphemes (e.g., *-ed*, *-s*, *-ing*, *-er*) in the spelling of children with reading and spelling disabilities (Bailet 1990; Invernizzi and Worthy 1989). Failure to spell inflections implies a failure of morphophonemic awareness. These endings are often not syllablic units (*begged*; *walked*) although they are morphological entities that are spelled consistently as if they were syllabic entities. Their pronunciation varies (/t/ or /d/, and /s/ or /z/) depending on phonemic context. Because they are spoken at the ends of words where speech sounds are more difficult to identify, and because they are linguistically complex, they may doubly tax the speech processing system at the phonological and morphological levels. On the basis of such evidence, linguistically oriented researchers have argued that a core deficit in dyslexia is insensitivity to both the phonological and morphophonological structure of words (Bailet 1990; Carlisle 1987; Fischer, Shankweiler, and Liberman 1985; Liberman et al. 1985). Students with spelling disabilities should be expected to make errors on words with inflections whose sound-spelling structure is complex and difficult to identify.

How are Phonological and Morphological Disorders Expressed in Spelling Errors?

For an observer to detect the influence of weak phonological processing on spelling, errors must be viewed in a more complex way than simple counting speech sounds represented. It is not the number of sounds spelled correctly that is of interest, or the number of words, but which words and phonemes produce error, and the speech sound environment in which those phonemes are misspelled. Simple phonetic accuracy in spelling can be achieved a number of different ways, with more or less closeness to standard spelling, and is not in itself very revealing of underlying linguistic processes. In the early stages of spelling development, a child may not know conventional symbols but will make spelling attempts that reflect an accurate perception of surface level phonetics. Spellings may look odd, or be impermissible according to orthographic rules, but they can be phonetically accurate if a child segments, sequences, and identifies the phonetic segments during spelling. Variations on the word *everything* may include AVETIG, AVRETING, EVVREY-THENG, and so forth; only one of these spellings, the omission of /r/ in the first word, is a misrepresentation of sound. The other choices confirm that the child is perceiving the phonemes, because the spellings are plausible using the child's system of phonology and knowledge of letters.

If dyslexia involves a subtle disorder of phonological processing, then those aspects of phonology that are inherently challenging for all learners should be the ones that expose the linguistic processing weaknesses in the dyslexic. Poor spellers, if their deficit is phonological in nature, should have trouble spelling the features of words that are least salient in articulation, more embedded in the syllable, or for some other reason difficult to segment and identify. A degraded or incomplete auditory image for a word in the phonological processor would be likely to cause faulty phoneme-grapheme mapping. The features of words being most prone to representational error would be those that are ambiguous in speech, those that are also difficult for normally developing learners.

On the basis of this articulatory salience hypothesis, end stop consonants and second consonants in clusters might be more difficult to spell than beginning consonants because they are unaspirated. Deaspiration of those consonants would make them more difficult to notice, identify, and remember. Later developing speech sounds, particularly liquids and fricatives, might be involved disproportionately in spelling errors. Unaccented vowels should be more subject to representational error than initial consonants or stressed vowels because their identity is ambiguous in spoken words. Other linguistic variables, such as morphophonemic complexity, grammatical class of a word, or word length might also be related to the likelihood of error.

Evidence for a Phonological Deficit in the Writing of Adolescents with Severe Spelling Disability

In a previous study (Moats in press), I analyzed all the spontaneous spelling errors of dyslexic adolescents in a series of written compositions produced during and after intensive remediation. Before that study was conducted, only the following limited evidence existed that poor spellers have relatively more difficulty representing specific phonological and morphophonological features of words in their spelling than comparison groups. I had found (Moats 1993) that 90% of a phonologically disordered high-school student's spelling errors could be classified as representing specific phonological errors; that student, who had experienced delayed development of /l/ and /r/ earlier in development, also made a high proportion of errors on liquids in spelling. In an unpublished study, Moats, Smith, and Haser (1992), compared third and fifth grade children with learning disabilities to normally progressing children at the same level of achievement. The students with spelling disabilities made proportionately more errors on consonant clusters and deletion of schwa vowels from unstressed syllables on nonsense-word spelling. Viise (1992) studied the orthographic knowledge of adults with low literacy, comparing them to younger students spelling at the same level. The adults with low literacy skills made comparatively more errors on inflections and deleted more unstressed syllables from multisyllablic words, although the general course of their spelling development followed the stages outlined by Henderson (1990) and his colleagues (Templeton and Bear 1992). Kibel and Miles (1994) recently reported that older dyslexic students made specific types of phonologically based errors on a small set of phonemes, including those that are late developing in speech and those that share articulatory features with other speech sounds. The "less noticeable phonemes in consonant clusters" and voiced/unvoiced consonant pairs were particularly vulnerable to error in their study. Given the convergence of such findings, it seemed probable that specific spelling errors in the spontaneous writing of adolescent dyslexic students should reflect their persistent difficulties with phonological awareness, phonological coding, and morphophonological awareness.

THE SPELLING ERRORS OF REMEDIATED ADOLESCENT DYSLEXICS

A Study of Errors in Spontaneous Writing

After considering the previous evidence, I subsequently carried out a descriptive study[1] to investigate the nature of persistent spelling problems in the spontaneous writing of older students with reading and spelling disabilities. The subjects had spent at least two years in an intensive, residential, specialized high school program for dyslexic students. Reading comprehension and expository writing, using established paragraph and thematic formats, was emphasized in the curriculum, along with multisensory, systematic methods for decoding and spelling. The study examined the possibility that spelling errors will reflect persistent phonological processing deficits if one looks at specific phonological phenomena. Spontaneous writing samples were analyzed because they are a natural expression of students' linguistic processing and linguistic knowledge, and are less contrived than dictated spelling tests, which may include words not in the students' writing vocabularies.

Subjects. The subjects in the study were 19 boys, all Caucasian, who had spent two or more years in a secondary residential school for dyslexic adolescents. All had been routinely tested with the Morrison-McCall graded spelling lists and a structured, expository writing assignment at the beginning, middle, and end of each year. Their typical age was 16 (range 14 to 17) at the time of the final writing sample and their typical grade placement was 11.7 (range 9.7 to 12.7). Full Scale IQ's ranged from 89 to 122. Spelling achievement varied from 1.5 grade equivalent to 7.0 grade equivalent upon entry into the school (x = 3.9),with the exception of one student on grade level. Word recognition (*Wide Range Achievement Test,* Jastak and Wilkinson 1984) varied from 2.8 to 7.8 (x = 4.9) upon school entry, with the exception of two able readers scoring at or above grade level. At the end of two years of instruction, spelling achievement ranged from 3.4 to 9.8 grade equivalent (x = 5.7) and word recognition had improved substantially in most subjects (x = 9.3).

Error Analysis Procedure. All spelling errors generated by each subject in beginning, middle, and end of the year essays were listed and categorized. The four most recent essays available for each subject—those that were most likely to show the effects of instruction—were used to obtain spelling data. These essays were to be examples of the students' best writing and were to follow the paragraph and essay formats emphasized in their English program. The topic, usually allowing personal and experiential writ-

---

[1]These data are also published in *Reading and Writing: An Interdisiplinary Journal,* 1996, special issue edited by J. Carlisle and D. Johnson of Northwestern University.

ing, was chosen by the writer from several titles offered, such as "The Perfect Age," "My Favorite Place," and "My Future Goals." No dictionaries or word processors were used for spelling correction.

The length of the compositions varied, with the average length being 105 words. The proportion of overall spelling inaccuracies ranged from 26%, or one word in four, to 1% for one of the best spellers. The five poorest spellers averaged a 13% error rate on their final compositions.

The focus of analysis was the nature of errors attributable to inaccurate phonological processing and inaccurate morphophonological processing. Inaccurate spellings that could be understood as errors of orthographic representation, those that represented the phonemes but that used incorrect letters, were also classified but not analyzed in so much detail. Thus, "orthographic errors" in this analysis were those that used the wrong symbols but that represented the speech sounds in some plausible manner, including the strategies often used by children at the immature phonetic spelling level. Overgeneralization of "silent e" was somewhat arbitrarily included in this category, as this phenomenon does not necessarily represent inaccurate processing of phonology. "Phonological errors," in contrast, were those that could be construed as omissions, substitutions, additions, or errors in the perception of speech sounds. Of special interest were spellings of the sonorants (liquids /l/ and /r/ and nasals /m/, /n/, and /J/) because sonorant consonants accounted for a high proportion of errors in the writing of first graders in Read's (1986) and Treiman's (1993) studies, and also in cases I have studied previously. "Morphophonological errors" were those that occurred on inflected morphemes. The categories of errors, with examples from the boys' writings, are listed in table 9.

TABLE 9:   CATEGORIES OF SPELLING ERRORS IN THE SPONTANEOUS WRITING OF ADOLESCENTS WITH DYSLEXIA

I. Orthographic (Phonologically Accurate) Errors:

A. Homophones:	BY/buy TO/two	THEN/than
B. Letter name strategies:	OPNING/opening	REFLXS/reflexes
C. Surface phonetic:	ONE/own TIPE/type	VOLY/volley CIND/kind
D.Failure to change root when ending was added:		HAVEING/having
		EASYER/easier
E. Student's pronunciation:	RESTERONT/restaurant	LUDGERY/luxury
F. Letter reversals:	EMDARASE/embarrass	
G. Schwa misspellings:	ATT<u>A</u>TUDE/attitude	PAR<u>A</u>NTS/parents
H. Overgeneralization of "silent e":	PLANE/plan LOTE/lot HOTELE/hotel	

II. Phonologically Inaccurate Spellings
   A. Errors on Nasals
      1. Omission of nasal after a vowel: KID/kind
      2. Omission of nasal after a liquid: LEARD/learned
      3. Omission of vowel + nasal: CLING/climbing
      4. Substitution of one nasal for another: MANBER/member
      5. Omission of entire "ing" ending[2]:   COME/coming
      6. Insertion of a nasal after a vowel: WOUNLD/would
      7. Other: KNOW/known
   B. Nasal-Liquid Substitution   AROULD/around
   C. Errors on Liquids /l/ and /r/
      1. Omissions of /l/ before consonants
        and after vowels: SEFE/self
      2. Inserting /r/ or /l/ before a vowel: WROK/work
      3. Omission of /r/ after a vowel: DEFENDO/defenders
      4. Omission of /l/ or /r/ in a blend: FENDS/friends
      5. Insertion of /r/ or /l/ after a vowel: CERPER/cheaper
      6. Omission of vowel + liquid: EVY/every
      7. Other: ONGUS/orange juice
   D. Omission of Non-sonorant Consonants
      1. Adjacent consonants across
        syllable boundaries: AFER/after
      2. Consonants within clusters: COOT/cost
      3. Medial syllable-initial: VEIO/video
      4. Word-final: POSITY/positive
   E. Consonant Substitutions   ME/be
   F. Consonant Additions   BELIEFT/belief
   G. Vowel Substitutions
      1. Stressed vowels: JOIB/job
      2. Unstressed vowels: RESIONS/reasons
      3. R-controlled vowels: WEREY/worry
   H. Deletion of Schwa: MANGED/managed
   I. Whole Syllable or Stressed Syllable Delete: COLORDO/Colorado
   J. Sequence: LOST/lots
   K. Word Substitutions: CLOSE/cost
   L. Multiple Errors, undecipherable: PROTILLY/prosperity?
III. Morphophonological Errors
   A. Morphophonological Errors on -ed
      1. Omit -ed: TALK/talked
      2. Phonetic sp. of -ed: HELPET/helped HAPEND/happened
      3. Addition of -ed: AFECTIVED/effective
      4. Other: SPSTOW/supposed to
   B. Morphophonological Errors on -s
      1. Plural /s/ on nouns omitted: GOAL/goals
      2. Verb/adverb markers omitted: SKI/skis
      3. Contractions with /s/ for "is":   THAT/that's
      4. Additions of noun/verb inflections: TEACHERS/teacher LEVES/leave
      5. Other: REASOND/reasons

---

[2]Omission of "ing" can be classified as both phonological and morphophonological. Only two errors were made in this category but they were noted in both classes.

Morphophonological errors included the omission, substitution, or phonetic spelling of inflected endings. Although phonetic spellings of inflections were accurate phonologically, they were noted because they indicated a failure to represent sound and meaning simultaneously. Past tense, plural, and possessive endings were of greatest interest because they bear a complex relationship to print, as previously noted. Categories of morphophonological errors are also shown in table 9.

Results. The 19 subjects, in spite of their placement in an intensive remedial school, varied in the nature of their spelling difficulties in spontaneous writing. As might be expected, phonological, morphophonological, and orthographic errors all occurred with diminishing frequency as spelling proficiency improved. There was no relationship between Verbal IQ, severity of spelling disorder, and rate of growth in spelling achievement in this group of subjects.

When the subjects were rank ordered by spelling achievement level on the final spelling test given at the end of two or more years of remediation they fell roughly into two groups: those who had progressed to a spelling level below a sixth grade equivalent ($n = 10$) and those who scored above a sixth grade level ($n = 9$). The group who never progressed beyond a sixth grade level, who scored between 3.5 and 5.8 in spelling achievement after intensive remediation, made many more errors, although the length of composition was approximately equivalent across groups. Subjects differed from one another within the low achieving group; some made a very high proportion of phonologically based errors, while others made fewer, but overall the frequency of errors suggesting phonological and morphophonological processing difficulties was highest for the poorer spellers, as shown in table 10.

TABLE 10 DIFFERENCES BETWEEN POORER AND BETTER SPELLERS ON FREQUENCY OF ORTHOGRAPHIC, PHONOLOGICALLY INACCURATE, AND MORPHOLOGICALLY INACCURATE SPELLINGS

	Poorer Spellers (n=10)	Better Spellers (n=9)
Total Orthographic (PA)	344 (54%)	124 (74%)
Total PI and MI	289 (46%)	43 (26%)
Total Errors	633	167

Note: *PA=phonologically accurate; PI=phonologically inaccurate; MI=morphologically inaccurate.*

Errors of Phonological Representation Made by the Poorer Spellers. Specific phonological error types that differentiated the poorer from the better spellers included a much higher rate of omissions, insertions, and subtitutions of sonorants (/l/, /r/, /m/, /n/, /ŋ/). In fact among the poor spellers, sonorant errors accounted for 24% of all the errors involving inaccurate phonological or morphophonological representation. Sonorant omissions were the most common error type, and the largest number of these occurred after a vowel and before a consonant. Of the 38 errors involving liquids /l/ and /r/, 18 of these occurred when the liquid followed a vowel and preceded a consonant. Nine more liquid errors involved misplacement of a liquid in relation to a vowel. There were no errors on either liquids or nasals when they were the first phoneme in a word.

Of the 29 errors involving the nasals /m/, /n/, and /ŋ/ in the poorest spellers, 12 occurred when the nasal followed a vowel and preceded a consonant. In both cases, omissions occurred as often on unstressed syllables as stressed syllables; stress did not appear to be a factor. By far the most often omitted or confused nasal phoneme was /n/. Twelve of 13 nasal omissions involved /n/. Four of 6 nasal substitutions involved an n replacing an m. Three of 4 insertions were of /n/.

Other errors of phonological representation occurring with high frequency in the poorer spellers were omissions of consonants from clusters across (9) and within (13) syllable boundaries, implausible substitutions of vowels (19), deletions of unstressed vowels (14) and stressed vowels (15), consonant substitutions (18), and whole word substitutions (28). Most consonant substitutions were not arbitrary but involved the use of a consonant that shared articulatory features with the target. For example, the alveolars /t/ and /d/ were substituted for each other between a stressed and unstressed syllable where they were reduced to flaps. Voiced/voiceless consonant pairs (NAGED/naked) were a frequent source of error, as were the phonemes spelled with digraphs sh, th, and ch. Vowel substitutions were also not arbitrary, but usually were made with vowels sharing general articulatory placement in front, medial, or back position, for example the letter "e" for /I/.

Morphophonological Errors of the Poorer Spellers. Morphophonologically inaccurate spellings were much more common among the poorer spellers. The frequency of errors on inflected endings -s and -ed was significantly higher among the poorer spellers than among the better ones (64 vs. 14). Of all the errors of phonological and morphophonological representation, inflection errors accounted for 23%. Omission of /s/ plural occurred very frequently among the lower achievers (27 of 35 /s/ deletions) but was quite uncommon in the misspellings of those attaining a sixth grade level or better (6). Omissions of -ed were also frequent among the poorer spellers (13); only 3 of these occurred with the /ɛd/ pronunciation, and the other 10 with non-syllabic -ed, equally divided between /d/ and /t/ pronunciations. The 9 better spellers omitted -ed only five times in all their writing. Other errors involved omission of /s/ verb markers, inappropriate additions of /s/, and substitutions of inflections for one another.

Differences between the Poorer and Better Spellers in Rate of Learning. When the students were rank ordered according to the gain in spelling achievement that had been made over two years, those with the highest proportion of phonological and morphophonological spelling errors, also the lower achievers, tended to improve the most slowly (about 1.4 years on average). Those with fewer phonological inaccuracies, the group who exceeded a sixth grade level of achievement, tended to improve the most rapidly (about 2.5 years on average). There were several exceptions to this trend, as would be expected on the basis of uncontrolled variables such as motivation and prior instructional history.

Most Commonly Misspelled Words. Certain frequently used words were often spelled incorrectly by the poorer spellers. Many of these appear on lists of "spelling demons" or high frequency words that are commonly misspelled by children (Fry, Fountoukidis, and Polk 1985). The frequent errors occurred on *their/there* (16), *your/you're* (10), *to/too* (10), *want* (9), *buy* (7), *friend* (7), *have to* (7), *when* (6), *where, were, really, know, every*, and *because* (5 each). Also the source of at least three misspellings were *something, than/then, would, which, what, until, through, some, other, of, my, from*, and *do*.

Discussion. Individuals with intractable spelling disabilities do produce specific errors of a phonological nature in their spontaneous writing. Many of the dominant error types can be explained in terms of faulty or incomplete processing of individual phonemes, phoneme sequences, and inflections with problematic phonetic characteristics. The spelling error patterns did suggest specific ways in which phonological insensitivity compromises the ability to spell. Specific errors occurred with much higher frequency than would be expected if a global "phonetic spelling" capability were impaired in these dyslexic learners. The spelling problems these learners exhibited was not one of *phonetic* representation, but one of faulty phonological and morphophonological processing. Their weaknesses in phoneme segmentation and identification were subtle enough to interfere selectively with the coding and/or retrieval of the less salient and more ambiguous linguistic elements in words.

All the subjects were receiving similarly designed, intensive instruction in decoding, spelling, and expository writing. The most prevalent error types were evidently resistant to remediation over several years of instruction. For many subjects, their learning curve for spelling had flattened by the end of high school. In spite of similar diagnoses and similar instructional background, the group was heterogeneous with regard to spelling proficiency, rate of spelling achievement gain, and prevalent type of error. The group of students who made better improvement (2.5 years of gain in spelling for 2.0 years of instruction on average) made many fewer errors of the phonological and morphophonological types in their writing. In general, the frequency of the three major error types, phonological, morphophonological, and ortho-graphic, decreased as students became better spellers.

The ten poorer spellers, who made the least progress in instruction and who remained below a sixth-grade level in spelling achievement, made a high proportion of errors on parts of words that were phonologically or mor-phophonologically ambiguous or complex. Almost half their total errors were poor phonological or morphophonological representations; almost half of those errors occurred with the misspelling of sonorants (liquids /l/, /r/; nasals /m/, /n/, /ŋ/). Interestingly, most misrepresentations of the sonorant phonemes occurred in the syllable segment known as the rime: the vowel and what comes after it (Treiman 1993). As Treiman reports, young normal children also frequently misspell sonorants after vowels in a rime. Yet most learn by sixth grade or so (Schlagal 1992) to resolve the ambiguity of vowel-sonorant combinations for spelling.

The adolescent dyslexic students in this study were developmentally delayed in that they remained unable to represent phoneme sequences or to differentiate confusable phonemes that are also difficult for younger chil-dren. However, their inability to resolve these confusions even after excel-lent instruction strongly suggests that degraded phonological codes may be a primary underlying cause of their enduring spelling difficulties. Dyslexic stu-dents might distinguish and remember an imperfect phonological code for phonetic spelling, and fail to attend to specific featural details of words. This problem, in turn, could limit the extent to which orthography can be mapped to phonology in the lexical coding system.

Morphophonological errors involving the omission, substitution, or confusion of inflections were common to all the poorer spellers, consistent with the findings of Bailet (1990). Deletion of plural /s/ was most common and clearly differentiated the poorer from the better spellers of this learning disabled group. Again, both the plural and the past tense segments are lin-guistically complex; they are usually not syllabic segments in speech. They occur at the ends of words and are not salient in articulation. Their phonetic realizations vary depending on the structure of the word to which they are added, but they are spelled consistently. The frequent omissions, substitu-tions, and misrepresentations of inflections also served to reveal the linguis-tic insensitivity of the poorer spellers.

The frequency of errors on certain high frequency sight words was also noteworthy. These words were almost all of Anglo-Saxon origin and employ improbable or unique spellings. In addition, they are largely function words: pronouns, conjunctions, auxiliaries, prepositions, and interrogatives. The in-ability of poor spellers to remember them suggests that underdeveloped phonological and linguistic awareness compromises the foundation on which graphemic memory is dependent. If graphemic memory could develop independently of phonology, poor spellers might remember these short, common words by rote or habit, even though their linguistic analysis abilities were impaired. This was not the case. Memory for these words appears to improve as phonological errors decrease. Perhaps an explicit realization of the phoneme structure of words is necessary to remember the ways in which some spellings are exceptional or different from what is expected.

IS THERE A VISUAL-ORTHOGRAPHIC SUBTYPE OF SPELLING DISABILITY?

The possibility of a specific, developmental orthographic memory or output deficit in spelling disability could be predicted on the basis of theoretical models of spelling (see Chapter 3, this volume, and Adams 1990; Ellis 1993; Hooper et al. 1993; Snowling, Stackhouse, and Rack l986; Stanovich 1992) that acknowledge the important role of the orthographic processor in remembering words. Certainly there are strong arguments for a visual-orthographic subtype of reading disability (Watson and Willows 1993). However, the manner in which a developmental orthographic deficit would express itself is still a matter of debate, and measurement of orthographic processing as a distinct subskill of reading and spelling is difficult. Case studies of adults with specific, acquired orthographic processing dysfunction (Caramazza et al. 1987; Hillis and Caramazza 1989; Postero, Zinelli, and Mazzucchi l988) have shown that in such cases, letter omissions increased as spelling words became longer (seven letters or more) and were more numerous than letter insertions, transpositions, and inversions. Letter deletions occurred most often in the middle of words. The adults with orthographic processing impairment were poor at writing to dictation, copying seven-letter words from memory, spelling orally, and writing names for objects, all of which theoretically rely on an orthographic memory buffer. The effect occurred on long words but not on short words, and there was no evidence for a specific phonological deficit in these individuals. Similar patterns of error were reported by Lecours (1966) in his interesting study of Lee Harvey Oswald's diary; 85% of Oswald's errors could be classified as representing an unstable orthographic image, in which letters were deleted, inserted, or reversed in sequence.

Like phonological processing ability, orthographic memory skill is probably distributed on a continuum and has multiple dimensions (Seymour 1994). As stated earlier, orthographic processing is a language-specific function, unrelated to non-linguistic, visual-spatial perception or memory . The visual-orthographic memory store must accumulate from exposure to print and includes all known spellings, not just irregular words (Adams 1990; Ehri 1989; Seidenberg and McClelland 1989). Phonological awareness and phoneme-grapheme mapping may provide the crucial underpinning for establishing the graphemic memory store (Rack, Snowling, and Olson 1992). Until a learner has at least a rudimentary awareness of the phoneme constituents of words, the graphemes that correspond to phonemes cannot be automatically associated. Therefore, a specific problem with graphemic memory might be difficult to detect until subjects have acquired competence in phoneme segmentation.

It has been known for a long time that poor readers are less sensitive to orthographic redundancy or repeating letter patterns and sequences than good readers (Schwartz and Doehring 1977) and seem to form less explicit and complete representations of letter sequences in the graphemic memory used for word recognition (Corcos and Willows 1993; Frith 1980a). Good readers who are poor spellers may also be unable to store the complete and elaborated images of words necessary for spelling recall, but the word memories may be sufficient for word recognition (Frith 1985). Therefore, it is likely that specific spelling disability, in the absence of reading disability, involves a specific dysfunction of orthographic processing.

In the following case (figure 6), the 17-year-old subject could read nonsense words without difficulty, could track speech sounds in one-syllable nonsense words without difficulty, and could spell phonetically predictable words that were short. However, his spelling was marked by letter deletions, substitutions, and insertions of letters, especially in medial four-letter strings. In addition, the letters most often involved in his errors were those which

Spellings produced at age 11, prior to intensive remediation. Underlined parts of words refer to letter deletions, sequential order confusions, or telescoping effect.

eq<u>mnp</u>t/equipment	gar<u>nth</u>/gathering
arond/around	w<u>arthe</u>/whether
fornt/forgotten	cumthing/something
dash<u>d</u>/dashed	gr<u>pane</u>/gripping
pa<u>rn</u>ce/performance	a<u>balganechen</u>/obligation
walckm/welcome	lis<u>nte</u>/listen

Age 17, after three intensive years in Orton-Gillingham tutorial program. 80% of errors involve orthographic deletions, sequential order confusions, or substitutions of letters occurring elsewhere in word. No errors on phonological awareness testing (auditory).

giv<u>ie</u>n/given	examians/examines
physi<u>cs</u>ion/physician	musicsion/musician
app<u>era</u>nce/appearance	quanty/quantity
ex<u>cu</u>tive/executive	opertunty/opportunity
con<u>cinces</u>/conscience	nesscisty/necessity
sha<u>l</u>ow/shallow	cur<u>tosty</u>/courtesy
ath<u>litic</u>/athletic	an<u>ixty</u>/anxiety
Austr<u>ia</u>la/Australia	

Figure 6. Case study W.F., with orthographic memory deficit. Good reader/poor speller, IQ 120.

tended to occur several times in a word. This same subject, at age 11, prior to intensive remediation with an Orton-Gillingham approach, was a poor reader who did not know phonic correspondences. His spellings at that time were poor phonetic representations and had a "telescoped" quality of shortness and letter deletion in medial position. The locus of this subject's spelling problem is most likely the graphemic memory store; his delayed phonological awareness and difficulty learning sound-symbol relationships was eventually remediated, but his ability to remember specific, detailed letter sequences remained impaired. This individual also was diagnosed with a mild attention deficit disorder. Possibly there is a strong link between orthographic production problems and ADD.

Automaticity

Many children with spelling disability may also be deficient in their ability to retrieve linguistic knowledge automatically. Their spontaneous writing may be error-ridden because they cannot attend to spelling while their attention is divided among the many cognitive dimensions of writing (Gerber 1986; Gerber and Hall 1987; Hooper et al. 1994). These students typically score low on tests of symbolic processing speed, and although they may show basic mastery of individual sound-symbol correspondences and single words, there is marked deterioration when they are given a composition to produce. These students find writing very tedious and frustrating.

SUMMARY

For children who are good spellers, children with spelling disabilities, and adults who are poor spellers, knowledge of spelling patterns unfolds along predictable developmental lines. The errors most children make show that certain aspects of spelling are inherently difficult for everyone, and that some patterns and correspondences are more obvious or easier to remember than others. Among the "normal" problems of average children and adults are difficulties learning vowel correspondences, problems remembering which letters should be doubled and when, and problems remembering spellings in which the vowel or syllable is indistinct or reduced in pronunciation. Individuals with spelling difficulties usually, but not always, have relatively greater difficulty with dimensions of spelling that make heavy demand on both phonological awareness and specific recall of letter sequences.

Phonological disabilities may be most debilitating in the earlier stages of spelling acquisition, and may be much less prominent in people with higher spelling achievement, higher verbal abilities, or a history of good instruction. Phonological disabilities do affect spelling in specific ways, by causing poor segmentation of the speech sounds in words and confusion about their identity.

Good readers who are poor spellers demonstrate subtle and specific problems with recall of letter sequences, as well as difficulty learning the complex spelling patterns that involve inflectional and derivational morphology. Their problems occur with more advanced and complex aspects of word structure, at a more advanced developmental plateau than individuals who are limited by their inability to make refined analyses of speech sounds.

Dyslexia or specific reading disability, assumed to include spelling disability, is usually defined in terms of poor decoding of nonsense words, inaccurate oral reading of text, and word reading below an arbitrary cut-point on a normal curve. Dyslexia could also be defined by the specific linguistic confusions that endure in children's spelling errors beyond the point where they are developmentally typical. These linguistic confusions, which are primarily phonological in nature, interfere with the development of spelling proficiency. The existence and prevalence of such errors suggests that phonological and morphophonological awareness should be taught to these students early on if they are to move beyond the natural barrier imposed by their limitations in linguistic analysis. The following chapter will review some approaches to assessment that can be helpful in determining what type of disorder a person presents and what type of intervention would be indicated, and the book will conclude with a review of specific instructional techniques.

CHAPTER 5

Assessment of Spelling[1]

ASSESSMENT FOR WHAT PURPOSE?

The purpose of an assessment will determine the approach selected to measure any academic performance area, including spelling proficiency. There is no one test available that will address all the purposes of assessment, which include: (a) determination of eligibility for special education services, (b) determination of developmental level of spelling proficiency in order to match instruction to the learner, (c) diagnosis of a specific type of learning disability (e.g., graphomotor output processing, phonological processing, or orthographic processing), and (d) evaluation of progress in response to instruction.

Spelling measurement is important to the differential diagnosis of oral language disorders, reading, written expression, and attention. Any person experiencing a developmental or acquired disorder of language is likely to show abnormalities of spelling. If the individual can spell well, the disorder probably does not involve the processing of language structure and may be limited to pragmatics (the communicative function of language). If the person spells poorly, there may be a global or specific language disorder or disorder of attention, in which case there is likely to be difficulty with related language skills, including speech sound segmentation in spoken words, short-term memory for novel words, nonsense word reading, or handwriting. Such individuals are likely also to have trouble with all forms of symbolization in writing, including the use of punctuation and capitalization.

WHAT IS IMPORTANT TO MEASURE?

An individual's written spelling accuracy may vary according to situational factors such as choice of writing topic, the amount of structure available in

---

[1]Much of this chapter was based on a previous publication, Moats (1994).

71

the writing task, level of motivation to produce a well-written product, and response mode (keyboarding, handwriting). Children with learning disabilities often "know" rules, patterns, or generalizations under structured conditions that they may not generalize to spontaneous writing. Because of this division between competence and performance, assessment should include both dictated tests and analysis of spelling in spontaneous writing. Thorough assessment should also include direct tests of related processing skills such as phonological analysis of words, handwriting speed and accuracy, recognition of orthographic patterns, and knowledge of specific sound-symbol relationships. Spelling should be compared to proficiency in written composition, reading decoding, reading comprehension, and mathematical calculation, in order to assess the broadness or specificity of a person's difficulty.

Below is a list of the functional domains important to assess, and examples of tests (or less formal evaluation methods) often used to assess those constructs:

> **Phonemic Awareness.** Lindamood Auditory Conceptualization Test (Lindamood and Lindamood 1979); Test of Auditory Analysis Skills (Rosner and Simon 1971); Test of Phonological Skills (Torgesen and Bryant 1994); informal tests of rhyming, Pig-Latin, phoneme counting.
>
> **Phonetic Spelling Ability.** Mann's (1993) or Tangel and Blachman's (1992, 1995) developmental scale to assess kindergarten and first-grade level students.
>
> **Alphabet Knowledge.** Informal assessment: have the student write the lower case cursive (or manuscript) letters from memory; write "forgotten" letters from dictation; name letters in an array; copy those letters that are not recalled at all. Record length of time required to write and copy. (See Berninger et al. 1992, for review of lower level skills in beginning writing).
>
> **Spelling Achievement Level.** Wide Range Achievement Test (Jastak and Wilkinson 1984); Wechsler Individual Achievement Test (Wechsler 1990); Test of Written Spelling-Revised (Larsen and Hammill 1986); Kaufman Educational Achievement Test (Kaufman and Kaufman 1985).
>
> **Developmental Level of Spelling Knowledge**. Qualitative Inventory of Spelling Development (Henderson 1990; Schlagal 1992).
>
> **Analysis of Errors.** Examine writing for errors that represent phonological and morphophonological confusions (see below).
>
> **Criterion-Referenced Assessment.** Spellmaster (Greenbaum 1987).
>
> **Reading Skill and Phonic Knowledge.** Woodcock Johnson Tests of Achievement Revised (Woodcock and Johnson 1989); Woodcock Reading Mastery Tests (Woodcock 1987); Decoding Skills Test (Richardson and DiBenedetto 1985).

Written Composition. Wechsler Individual Achievement Test (Wechsler 1991); Test of Written Language-2 (Hammill and Larsen 1988); Written Language Assessment (Grill and Kirwin 1989); Woodcock-Johnson Tests of Achievement-Revised (Woodcock and Johnson 1989).

WHAT MAKES A GOOD TEST?
Representative Sampling of the Spelling Domain

Valid measures of spelling knowledge should meet several important criteria. First, a test should sample the whole domain of spelling if it purports to be a broad-based measure of spelling achievement. The domain of orthographic patterns, sound-symbol correspondences, and morphological constructions in English is very large, and includes often-ignored entities such as contractions, homophones, compounds, Latin plurals, and assimilated prefixes. As reviewed in Chapter 1, English orthography is a largely rule-governed and predictable system, but spelling structure can be linguistically complex. Tests that divide words in "predictable" and "unpredictable" (e.g., *The Test of Written Spelling-Revised*, Larsen and Hammill 1986; *The Wechsler Individual Achievement Test*, Wechsler 1991) treat the language in an overly simplistic way and will be of limited use in diagnosing and teaching individuals. The predictability of English spelling is a matter of degree, and necessitates consideration of several levels of language organization (phonology, orthography, morphology, meaning, and word origin).

Truly unpredictable words, those with unique spellings of two or more graphemes which are not predictable by phoneme-grapheme correspondence rules, are unusual and make up about 10 to 15% of the language at most. Words become unpredictable when they do not have enough companions in the dictionary to form a redundant pattern. Some redundant patterns violate phoneme-grapheme rules but are predictable because they are common, such as the *ild, old, ind, ost* patterns; some correspondences work for whole syllables such as tion and cial; and some spellings are predictable if the word's origin or the word's meaning are considered (*chorus; mosquito; cassette*). Many of our most common words are exception words. The most frequent of these tend to be old Anglo-Saxon words whose pronunciations have changed radically over centuries[2]. Of the 100 most often used words given in one list (Fry, Fountoukidis, and Polk 1985) about one-fourth have frankly "irregular" consonant or vowel spellings, including:

---

[2]See Balmuth (1992) for a full discussion of the historical changes in pronunciation that have led to the discrepancies between modern speech and older writing conventions, especially for words originating from Anglo Saxon.

of	to	you	was
as	they	have	from
word	what	were	your
do	other	many	some
two	could	people	water
come	there	their	are
one	said	would	been

Although it is important to include a sample of these most common words in any spelling assessment, loading a test with them may skew results. A balance needs to be maintained when a test is designed, including items that sample the complete domain of spelling in a balanced manner. The content domain from which we can sample a student's spelling knowledge and skills is outlined in table 11.

Sufficient Coverage at Each Developmental Level

Tests become unreliable when there are not enough items to sample an individual's skill at the person's level of development. For example, test scores that are based on two or three items are unreliable. That is why it is necessary to supplement many norm-referenced achievement tests with an appropriately selected list of words at the person's instructional level. In addition, any qualitative analysis of errors will be most valid if it is performed using words at the person's instructional level (Morris, Nelson, and Perney 1986).

Representativeness or Ecological Validity

An ecologically valid test is one that is representative of what children are expected to learn or do in school. Thus, it would be foolish to include words on a spelling test that children almost never use in their own writing or never have seen in reading (e.g., *yacht*) unless the purpose was to test their ability to spell unfamiliar or nonsense words. It is also useless to give a test of proofreading ability or one that has multiple choice answers and hope to make inferences about written spelling generated by the student. Although multiple choice tests do correlate fairly well with dictated tests, there is no possibility for meaningful error analysis with a proofreading format.

Meeting Standard Psychometric Properties

If measures used for assessing achievement have concurrent validity (adequate correspondence with other accepted measures), are adequately normed, and have demonstrated reliability (can be counted on to yield the same score if the test could be repeated) they can be used for classification and eligibility decisions. Unfortunately, there are tests in common use that do not meet these standards and that should be avoided.

TABLE 11: OUTLINE OF CONTENT DOMAIN IN ENGLISH SPELLING.

I.	*Phoneme-Grapheme Correspondences*	*Examples*
	A. Predictable Spellings	
	1. consonants	h*i*m, na*p*kin
	2. vowels	w*e*t, pi*c*nic
	3. consonant blends	*fl*ag, *dr*agon
	4. consonant digraphs	*ch*in, fi*sh*
	B. Variant/Conditional Correspondences	
	1. consonants	dre*ss*, e*dg*e, re*s*ult
	2. vowels	gr*ow*n, l*igh*t, expl*ai*n
	3. blends	bli*nk*, s*qu*are, s*c*ary
	4. digraphs	whi*ch*, ki*tch*en
II.	Syllable Patterns	
	A. Closed (CVC)	*si*ster, Se*p*tember
	B. Open (CV)	*be*hind, *no*body
	C. R-controlled	fi*re*, p*or*ter, c*are*
	D. C-le	bu*gle*, treat*able*
	E. VCe	*base*ment, com*pile*
	F. Vowel Team	h*au*nted, t*rea*sure
	G. special syllables	a*ction*, atom*ic*
III.	Orthographic Rules	
	A. -ve	have, give, love
	B. f,l,s doubling	less, stiff, pull
	B. doubling final consonant	running, fogged
	C. change y to i	studious, beautiful
	D. drop silent e	baked, coming
IV.	Inflections	walked, wanted; dogs, wishes quickly, using, highest
V.	Silent Letters	sign-signal; bomb-bombard
VI.	Irregular (Odd) Spellings	of, one, enough, friend, said
VII.	Homophones	their, there; to, two, too
VIII.	Compounds	breakfast, fifty-one
IX.	Affixes (Latin-based)	predict, protection vision, enjoyment attend, appearance
X.	Greek Combining Forms	microscope, psychobiology
XI.	Contractions	you've, I'll, don't
XII.	Possessives, Plurals	night's; oxen; alumnae, crises
XIII.	Abbreviations	etc.; St.; p.m.
XIV.	Alternation Patterns	mischief-mischievous explain-explanation define-definition serene-serenity

NORM-REFERENCED ACHIEVEMENT TESTS

There is no perfect test of spelling commercially available; each of those reviewed here has short comings and strengths. Very few norm-referenced tests attempt inclusively to sample the domain of spelling. For example, the *Wide Range Achievement* spelling subtest (Jastak and Wilkinson 1984), frequently used in learning disabilities research, contains no irregular forms, no inflected words or words that follow orthographic change rules for adding endings, no contractions, compounds, possessives, or plurals. The sampling of consonant blends, digraphs, and diphthongs appears to be unsystematic, although most vowels are represented on the word list. Of the norm-referenced spelling tests on the market designed to measure spelling achievement levels, several do meet minimum standards for reliability and concurrent validity. These include the *Test of Written Spelling—2* (Larsen and Hammill 1986) the *Kaufman Test of Educational Achievement* (Kaufman and Kaufman 1985), the *Wide Range Achievement Test—Revised* (Jastak and Wilkinson 1984) and the spelling subtest from the *Wechsler Individual Achievement Test* (Wechsler 1991). *The Woodcock-Johnson Tests of Achievement—Revised* (Woodcock and Johnson 1989) also measures spelling with a combination of word dictation and proofreading items. The technical characteristics of such tests have been reviewed elsewhere (Bain, Bailet, and Moats 1991; Bradley-Johnson and Lesiak 1989; Conoley and Kramer 1989; Mitchell 1985), but a few more comments about these commonly used measures are in order.

The *Test of Written Spelling-Revised* purports to have content validity because of its two "predictable" and "unpredictable" word lists based on the Hanna et al. (1966) study. This dichotomous classification is a dubious one, as previously discussed. The inclusion of some words on the "unpredictable" list is puzzling (*much, yes, she*), because these words are spelled phonetically if not according to orthographic rule (for example, *much* by rule would be *mutch*, and *yes* would be *yess*). The absence in both lists of complex linguistic structures such as inflected endings is notable. More importantly, there is no evidence presented in the manual that these two lists of words measure independent spelling abilities; in fact, the correlation between the two lists is very high in the standardization sample, perhaps mitigating the need for two lists. Apparently, children with good phonological skills and poor orthographic processing are presumed to spell predictable words more accurately than unpredictable words, and children with phonological processing impairments are presumed to spell unpredictable words better than predictable words. However, there is no evidence that children with spelling disabilities respond differently to these lists more often than non-disabled children, or that differences in performance on the lists characterize subtypes that respond differently to instruction. In studies directly investigating this question, children with phonological impairments have been found to do poorly on both types of words, and children with good phonological processing have been found to do well on both types of words (Stuart and Masterson 1992). The total test score on the TWS-2 may be reliable for classification purposes, but more refined diagnosis of disability should be undertaken with supplementary instruments.

The Kaufman Test of Educational Achievement provides a format for error analysis of prefixes, suffixes, syllable patterns, vowel spellings, and consonants, although only two or three examples of each pattern are included for analysis. There are not enough items to measure lower level (first-grade) spelling skills reliably. The sample of words does not include many linguistic constructions or oddities, but the test's psychometric properties with respect to standardization and reliability are preferable to those of its competitors.

The *Woodcock-Johnson-Revised*, while including items that cover the domain of spelling much more broadly than the other tests, contains too few items at lower developmental levels to be precise or sensitive to smaller increments of change. It does not yield enough information to support qualitative analyses of error types.

The new *Wechsler Individual Achievement Test*, in addition to offering recent and comprehensive normative data, offers a word list deliberately constructed with regular words, irregular words, and homonyms. Although the overall domain of words included is an improvement on the WRAT-3, the three-part classification is simplistic and problematic. The range of the test is good in that there appear to be an adequate number of words at the lower and upper levels to give meaningful information about very poor and very good spellers.

Because of the absence of theoretically driven word selection and restricted sampling at each level of development, these tests have limited potential for illuminating the linguistic processing factors that may be significant in spelling disability, but each may be useful as a power test of achievement level.

DEVELOPMENTAL ANALYSIS OF SPELLING
Measuring Qualitative Change in Early Spelling Development

Spelling achievement tests, such as those reviewed above, lack precision and reliability when the range of words young children know is limited. Of primary interest in the early stages of learning to spell is how closely a child can approximate a spelling of an unknown word, using phonemic analysis and their knowledge of letters. Scoring systems designed to be sensitive to changes in developmental level in early spelling were introduced by several investigators (Liberman et al. 1985; Mann, Tobin, and Wilson 1987) and recently validated by Mann (1993) and Tangel and Blachman (1992, 1995). These investigators have devised quality point systems for determining developmental level of spelling in children at kindergarten and first grade. Mann (1993; Mann et al. 1987) selected words for the spelling test to elicit preconventional spelling strategies. This list is as follows:

thank you	people	men	dog
angry	girl	color	red
bed	name	lady	boy
fish	boat		

The stimuli were selected to include the presence of a letter name in the word (*thank you, people*); short vowels (*bed, red, men, fish, dog*); nasals before stop consonants (*thank you, angry*); liquids (*girl, color*), and consonant digraphs (*fish*); and tense vowels or diphthongs (*name, lady, boat, boy*), all of which elicit predictable phonetic spelling responses in beginning writers. Words with affricated initial consonants (*trick or treat, dragon*) could also have been included.

Tangel and Blachman (1992, 1995) chose five words to give their kindergarteners (*lap, sick, elephant, pretty,* and *train*). They added five more for their first graders (*hunt, street, kissed, order, snowing*). These more advanced words deliberately included a preconsonantal nasal, a 3-consonant cluster, an r-controlled vowel, and two inflections. Tangel and Blachman demonstrated the high reliability of their scoring system. Quality points were assigned according to the progressive improvements children were expected to make on the basis of developmental theory. A general set of criteria was as follows:

Points	Criteria	Example
0 pts.	no alphabetic representation, random symbols	xopqr
1 pt.	initial phoneme represented with phonetically related letter, or other single letter representing a salient part of the word	r/lap k/sick
2 pts	correct initial phoneme, may be followed by random letter string	stuv/sick

3 pts	more than one phoneme but not all, with phonetically related or conventional letters	sowe/snowing
4 pts	all phonemes, with mix of phonetically related or conventional letters	chran/train
5 pts.	all phonemes with conventional letters; correct short vowel; attempt to mark long vowel	snoing/snowing
6 pts.	correct spelling	

A measure of this type given at the end of kindergarten appears to be a very strong predictor of reading ability at the end of first grade. It reflects the effect of phoneme awareness training and spelling instruction. How long the measurement strategy would provide useful documentation of developmental changes in beginning spellers or children with spelling disabilities is not known. The next approach to qualitative analysis is fruitful once children have begun formal spelling instruction or can spell at a late first-grade level.

The Qualitative Inventory of Word Knowledge

A useful tool for surveying the developing orthographic knowledge of children is the Qualitative Inventory of Word Knowledge developed at the University of Virginia (Henderson 1990; Schlagal 1992) (table 12). This instrument is used routinely at the McGuffey Reading Center and is extremely helpful in finding a child's instructional level for spelling. This instrument is particularly useful for demonstrating the broad range of spelling skills within any single classroom and helping teachers understand that some children will not learn as efficiently if they are made to memorize words that are beyond their instructional readiness (Morris et al. in press). The lists do not take long to give, and can be given to a group. The inventory consists of six word lists drawn from a larger pool of words used to construct basal spelling books for each grade level. Concurrent validity has been established (Schlagal 1992), as well as the instrument's reliability in distinguishing spelling instructional level (Morris, Nelson, and Perney 1986; Henderson 1990). The word lists represent both the underlying structural order in the orthography and the developmental progression of children's concepts about print. They include high frequency Anglo-Saxon words at the beginning levels, and lower frequency words of Latin and Greek origin which embody complex relationships between sound, meaning, and spelling patterns at the higher levels.

As a general guideline, 90% accuracy on a list constitutes independent functioning at that level; 50 to 89% constitutes instructional level function-

TABLE 12: QUALITATIVE INVENTORY OF SPELLING
DEVELOPMENT (Henderson, E. 1990. *Teaching Spelling*. Houghton Miflin. Reproduced by permission.)

I	*II*	*III*	*IV*	*V*	*VI*
girl	traded	send	force	lunar	satisfied
want	cool	gift	nature	population	abundance
plane	beaches	rule	slammed	bushel	mental
drop	center	trust	curl	joint	violence
when	short	soap	preparing	compare	impolite
trap	trapped	batter	pebble	explosion	musician
wish	thick	knee	cellar	delivered	hostility
cut	plant	mind	market	normal	illustrate
bike	dress	scream	popped	justice	acknowledge
trip	carry	sight	harvest	dismiss	prosperity
flat	stuff	chain	doctor	decide	accustom
ship	try	count	stocked	suffering	patriotic
drive	crop	knock	gunner	stunned	impossible
fill	yard	caught	badge	lately	correspond
sister	chore	noise	cattle	peace	admission
bump	angry	careful	gazed	amusing	wreckage
plate	chase	stepping	cabbage	reduction	commotion
mud	queen	chasing	plastic	preserve	sensible
chop	wise	straw	maple	settlement	dredge
bed	drove	nerve	stared	measure	conceive
	cloud	thirsty	gravel	protective	profitable
	grabbed	baseball	traffic	regular	replying
	train	circus	honey	offered	admitted
	shopping	handle	cable	division	introduction
	float	sudden	scurry	needle	operating
			camel	expression	decision
			silent	complete	combination
			cozy	honorable	declaration
			graceful	baggage	connect
			checked	television	patient

90% correct on a level represents mastery.
50-75% correct is the child's instructional level.
Below 50% correct is the child's frustration level—too difficult for direct instruction.

ing; and scores below 49% constitute frustration level functioning. The quality or accuracy of children's errors has been shown both by Schlagal (1992) and Morris et al. (1986) to deteriorate at a child's frustration level. Both these studies emphasize that error analysis is valid within the range of a child's tacit word knowledge, but not at the frustration level, because overwhelmed children make non-strategic guesses at words that are often uninterpretable.

While the Qualitative Inventory is very useful in evaluating students' instructional level in relation to a basal scope and sequence, it does not include high frequency irregular words, homonyms, contractions, possessives and plurals, all of which pose grave difficulty for persons with spelling disabilities.

INFERRING UNDERLYING PROCESS DEFICITS FROM SPELLING ERRORS
The Boder Method

The procedures of Boder and Jarricho (1982) have often been used in neuropsychological research to classify children by subtype according to their reading and spelling patterns. Boder (1973) asserted that dyslexic students spelled correctly fewer than half of words they could read at their instructional level, and that their error types allowed them to be classified as *dysphonetic*, *dyseidetic*, or *mixed*. Dysphonetic children had difficulty using phonic decoding skills and spelled most words with poor phonetic equivalents; dyseidetic children spelled most words with good phonetic equivalents but were slow at sight word recognition and recall of irregular words in spelling. In spite of this approach's popularity, it presents some major theoretical and procedural problems.

Scores are based on the percentage of predictable and unpredictable unknown words taken from the reading test that are spelled as good phonetic equivalents. Reliability may be reduced by the fact that each child takes a different spelling test composed by the examiner from the results of the reading test. The normative sample of 3,000 children is inadequately described. The test does not meet standards for test-retest reliability (Felton and Wood 1989). Both the "dysphonetic" and "dyseidetic" subtypes have linguistic processing deficits (Felton and Wood 1989; Olson 1985) when sensitive measures are used to diagnose them. The "dyseidetic" group demonstrates deficits in rapid automatic naming, similar to the rate-delayed group in Lovett's (1987) and Wolf's (1986) dyslexia research (Flynn et al. 1992). Slow naming processes, characteristic of many dyslexic children, in turn seem to be exacerbated by attention deficit disorder (Felton and Wood 1989), which overlaps considerably with the subtype designated to be dyseidetic. Finally, it is possible that both proficient and nonproficient spellers may vary along these same dimensions of phonetic accuracy and orthographic memory (Bryant and Impey 1986; Moats 1983; Stanovich 1992), and the subtypes may not be exclusively associated with a learning disorder. Better validation studies as well as substantial test revision and norming should be undertaken before the Boder test is used clinically.

The subtypes of Boder may very well represent either developmental stages in spelling acquisition, specific responses to the types of words selected for the test, or individual variation in global linguistic processing abilities (Miles and Miles 1991). Individuals with global language deficits or low Verbal IQ tend to make more dysphonetic errors than brighter or more verbally able children (Sweeney and Rourke 1985). Within the range of average Verbal IQ, children's phonetic accuracy changes significantly over time in the dyslexic population, as discussed in Chapter 4.

Direct Analysis of Spelling Errors

The major problem that arises with error analysis is the fact that many errors have several plausible explanations. For example, the spelling CAERFUL/ *careful* might be scored by one observer as a letter sequence error, by another as a "transitional" but phonetically accurate error, and by another as an orthographically "illegal" error because "ae" is not a permissible spelling for "long a" in English. A valid approach does not attempt to force errors into categories such as legal or illegal, or as phonetic or dysphonetic, because these are false dichotomies. Rather, it attempts to explain why certain elements of word structure are spelled the way they are by children or by adults with spelling difficulties, based on inherent linguistic properties in words and the principles of spelling and language development.

Phonological analysis, in contrast to phonetic analysis, considers the degree to which a spelling matches the spoken features of the entire word. A phonological error analysis needs to be informed by knowledge of written language, knowledge of child phonology, and knowledge of spelling development (Hoffman and Norris 1989). As suggested in the studies reported in the previous chapter, specific difficulties for individuals with phonologically based spelling disabilities include:

1. confusion, omission of vowel + sonorant (/l/, /r/, /r/, /m/, /ng/) in a syllable peak

CONMM/common WOSUT/wasn't EGGTOWN/Edgartown
PSN/person DRTER/daughter CLOL/color

2. substitution of consonant phonemes that share features such as voicing

STASUN/station RELTIFH/relatives TOGETTER/together

3. omission of consonants in blends or in non-salient positions

IELN/island POTET/protect AN/and

4. substitution of vowel phonemes that share features

MERRED/married PEK/pick

5. omission of unaccented (schwa) vowels or syllables

RELTIFH/relatives

6. omission or confusion of inflections *-ed* and *-s*

TAKT/talked DRESS/dresses

Individuals with spelling disability also are purported to have greater difficulty remembering words whose spellings involve complex relationships between morphology, phonology, and orthography (Bailet 1990; Bailet and Lyon 1985; Carlisle 1987; Fischer, Shankweiler, and Liberman 1985; Johnson 1986; Read and Ruyter 1985). Carlisle's (1987) word lists were organized to contrast older students' spellings of four types of derived words: those with no change of the base when endings were added; those with orthographic changes; those with phonological changes in the base; and those with both phonological and orthographic changes in the base. Examples of these are in table 13.

TABLE 13.   EXAMPLES OF WORDS USED IN STUDY OF MORPHOLOGICAL KNOWLEDGE (CARLISLE 1987).

No Change of Base Form in the Derived Form

enjoy	enjoyment
care	careful
usual	usually
perform	performance
profit	profitable

Orthographic Change in the Base Form to Create the Derived Form

swim	swimming
dense	density
happy	happiness
continue	continuance
propel	propeller

Phonological Change Made in the Base Form to Create Derived Form

human	humanity
drama	dramatic
magic	magician
discuss	discussion
sign	signal

Both Phonological and Orthographic Change Occurs in Base Form to Create Derived Form

type	typical
combine	combination
expand	expansion
decide	decision
admit	admission
produce	production

Not surprisingly, the words involving phonological changes between the base and derived word forms were the hardest for sixth through ninth graders to spell, and were relatively more difficult for ninth grade learning disabled subjects than other types of words.

Fischer, Shankweiler, and Liberman's (1987) study of adult poor spellers again showed that words with complex morphophonemic structures were the ones that elicited significant differences between the disabled and nondisabled subjects. The words lists employed in that study, useful for screening adults, are in table 14.

TABLE 14. EXAMPLES OF WORDS FOR TESTING LINGUISTIC SENSITIVITY IN ADULTS (FISCHER, SHANKWEILER, AND LIBERMAN 1985).

Words with Transparent Phoneme-Grapheme Structure ("Predictable")

yam	blunder	mask
inflate	clustering	retort
adverb	frustrated	preventive
vortex	stimulation	punishment

Words with Complex Morphophonemic Structure

unperceived	basically	flier
echoes	thinned	definitely
misspell	defensible	perferring
indigestible	utterance	grammar

Words with Unique or Orthographically "Irregular" Spellings

sergeant	eunuch	mnemonic
Wednesday	bourgeois	laugh
indebted	tongue	folk
pygmy	plagiarism	soldered
subpoena	hemorrhage	answering

Orthographic Processing Errors

Orthographic memory deficits may be most visible in spelling errors as subjects become older and have learned to spell phonetically. Orthographic memory errors may be most evident on longer words and may involve deletions, substitutions, and additions of letters, particularly in medial position (Bodecker, Hillis, and Caramazza 1990; Caramazza et al. 1987; Postero, Zinelli, and Mazzucchi 1988). Errors involving mental placekeeping of letters are not necessarily straightforward examples of sequence reversals, but may involve deletions and misplacements. Proposed error types in this domain are shown in table 15.

TABLE 15. PROPOSED CRITERIA FOR CLASSIFYING ERRORS AS VISUAL-ORTHOGRAPHIC. EXAMPLES FROM CASE STUDIES W.F. AND T.Z.

---

1. addition of a letter already present in a word
      lucidtity/lucidity   givien/given

2. deletion of a letter occurring elsewhere in a word
      physican/physician   medivel/medieval   excutive/executive

3. substitution of a letter with a letter already occurring in the word
      oppurtunity/opportunity   sholow/shallow

4. inversion of letter order
      exeragrate/exaggerate   locquious/loquacious   chartlean/charlatan
      eqmnpt/equipment   Austriala/Australia

MEASUREMENT OF RESPONSE TO INSTRUCTION

Spellmaster (Greenbaum 1987) is a published set of criterion-referenced tests designed for individualizing spelling instruction within a classroom group. It includes a series of diagnostic tests for assessing specific knowledge about spelling rules, patterns and generalizations, and knowledge of both homonyms and irregular words, and a manual to guide individualized instruction based on the diagnostic system. More comprehensive and detailed than the *Qualitative Inventory of Spelling Knowledge*, it is an excellent device for organizing an individualized classroom spelling program and measuring progress in retaining specific concepts about words and specific word lists.

Increase in correct bigram sequences, especially when small improvements in orthographic memory for less predictable or odd words is of interest, has been used to reflect response to instruction over the short term (Deno, Marston, and Mirkin 1982; Vaughn, Schumm, and Gordon 1992; White and Haring 1980).

How well a student is generalizing word list learning into spontaneous writing may be difficult to measure directly, but can be accomplished by keeping a running list of words commonly misspelled in a student's writing, and checking when the word is spelled correctly in a composition. Usually, three correct writings in a row constitute mastery learning. Comparing spelling in dictated lists with spelling in dictated passages could be a strategy for controlled measurement of automaticity or rapid recall of previously learned words. When generalization of a spelling rule or pattern is at issue, nonsense word spelling may be informative. Subjects' ability to profit from changes in linguistic input or mediating strategy (e.g., speaking the base word before spelling the derived; reminding subjects to say the word to themselves as they spell; pronouncing the word by syllables; segmenting the phonemes before spelling; mechanically slowing down or exaggerating the speech input) would be suitable for dynamic assessment. The possible effect of text manipulations (e.g., color coding; varying letter size or font) on orthographic memory for spelling is worthy of experimentation as well.

SUMMARY

Spelling assessment can be much more complex than simple administration of a norm-referenced test. Spelling errors can be analyzed to determine if a student is having difficulty with phonemic analysis, morphemic awareness, or recall of specific orthographic patterns. Spelling can be assessed from the perspective of developmental maturity and readiness for instruction. It is an important component in any diagnostic evaluation of a person with suspected learning disorders.

CHAPTER 6

Principles of Spelling Instruction[1]

REGULAR CLASSROOM PRACTICES

Through the earlier part of the twentieth century, spelling instruction research focused on classroom teaching and addressed several major questions:
Should word lists be grouped according to word frequency or word pattern?
What kind and what amount of practice will result in the most efficient and
generalizable learning? What role should tests play in word study? How can
teachers ensure that word study generalizes to writing? Although intervention studies of spelling instruction prior to 1980 typically did not define or
group their subjects according to their spelling level or their cognitive characteristics, several findings emerged consistently (Fitzsimmons and Loomer
1977; Hillerich 1985; Horn 1969):

1. The test-study-test method is desirable, especially if students immediately correct pretests themselves and use the information to focus
   their study.
2. Ten to fifteen minutes per day is sufficient for most students to
   master a week's spelling lesson of twenty words.
3. Words should be grouped by both frequency and spelling pattern.
4. Practice should include frequent writing of the unknown words,
   since spelling improves most when children are asked to write often.
5. Active study involving writing, analyzing, and categorizing words
   rather than "looking the words over" gets the best results.

Within currently popular "whole language" philosophies, *component
skill* development often takes the back seat (indeed, the rumble seat) in cur-
riculums that overemphasize composition to the detriment of handwriting,
spelling, punctuation, and grammar. Systematic, structured, and sequential

---

[1]This chapter has been published in somewhat altered form as Spelling: A Window on Linguistic Development,
in *Teaching Reading: Language, Letters, and Thought*, ed. S. Brody, Milford, NH: LARC Publishing, 1994

spelling instruction is often not emphasized in such programs because it is viewed as a distraction from a focus on authentic, meaningful written expression. Unfortunately, many teachers have been led to believe that children will "naturally" acquire spelling knowledge when they can read and if they are given sufficient writing practice. In such a climate, children with spelling difficulties are often left to flounder on their own, or are assigned to a learning specialist who may attempt to teach decoding and spelling with little reinforcement from the classroom program. In these situations, children with typical learning abilities also miss the opportunity to learn about the structure of language. Children whose program depends entirely on expressive writing and who are encouraged to "invent" spelling as they go along frequently establish incorrect habits for common words that are then difficult to change.

INSTRUCTION FOR GOOD SPELLERS

Some children learn to spell rather effortlessly, but they do nevertheless need instruction. Such children easily remember orthographic patterns as they encounter them in print. They also do well on tests of phonological processing, because the ability to discriminate and analyze speech sounds is a prerequisite for spelling competence as well as decoding proficiency. Children with good spelling memories can learn by any organized method, as long as some type of systematic practice is present, and the spelling list is at the appropriate level developmentally.

Basal programs, designed for use by grade level with large classes of students, vary considerably from one another and need to be used with caution. Many contain information that is not linguistically accurate. Some provide wasteful "busywork" practice, and often provide no valid rationale for including words on lists. Sometimes they oversimplify or explain poorly the complexities of sound-symbol correspondence. Because they are designed for the average child at a given grade level, the instructional level and unique needs of less able learners (and the most able learners) typically are not met. Too many words and too many concepts are presented at once, too many confusable stimuli are offered in one lesson, and not enough review and practice of previously learned material is offered for the poor speller. Further, basal texts often fail to give the linguistic or historical reasons English words are spelled the way they are, when such information might help spelling make sense.

Basal texts can be useful for average children if the level of difficulty is matched to the students' developmental spelling level, using a developmental assessment (see Chapter 5) and if the teacher follows the research-supported steps listed above. Within any typical classroom, several levels of spelling ability will need to be addressed simultaneously, because many children will be either above or below grade level. One of the most critical factors in the success of such an approach is the teacher's ability to direct students' attention to various aspects of word structure. Teachers must therefore be devoted students of language study themselves.

INSTRUCTION FOR POOR SPELLERS

What can be done for the person who spells poorly? Too often, the poor speller in the elementary grades is deemed not ready for instruction; the poor speller in the intermediate grades is deemed unresponsive to instruction; and the poor speller in high school or beyond is viewed as a hopeless case. Because such attitudes prevail, it is not surprising that poor spellers often remain untaught. Although research on general classroom instruction of spelling is plentiful, research on spelling instruction for the student with well-defined spelling disability is much more limited.

Spelling improvement can be brought about in poor spellers if proper instruction is carried out systematically over a long period of time (see Chapter 4), and the spelling instruction is tailored to match the developmental level of the student's word knowledge (Invernizzi, Abouzeid, and Gill 1994; Morris et al. in press). Very poor spellers seldom progress in spelling as fast as they can improve in reading. Although the ultimate gains may be modest, they provide a basis for simple written communication. An effective instructional program for poor spellers, according to criteria of the National Teacher Education Task Force of The Orton Dyslexia Society, will be integrated with other language instruction and will include the following components:

- Direct teaching with teacher-student interaction.
- Simultaneous, multisensory methodology.
- Systematic, sequential, and cumulative emphasis on phonology.
- Synthetic-analytic phonics progressing from part to whole.
- Systematic morphology for spelling and usage.

Teacher-directed, systematic practice with controlled amounts of new information

Systematic teaching regulates the amount of information presented to the learner at one time, the number of concepts or patterns (amount of redundancy) present in the stimuli, and the amount of practice that occurs with new and old information. The teacher assumes that forgetting will occur, making new learning difficult to establish. Instruction is carried out with the aid of careful record keeping to determine when words, patterns, and concepts are learned.

Why is it necessary to be systematic? One reason is the exact nature of what must be learned. Children who cannot spell well obviously do not remember words from incidental exposure to print. Spelling requires explicit and precise recall of orthographic sequences. The correspondence system is less predictable for spelling than it is for reading, so that greater demands are placed on word-specific orthographic memory in spelling. In addition, many of the most commonly used words in English are of Anglo-Saxon origin and have retained low frequency or odd spellings that also must be memorized, even though they are in part predictable (see Appendix A).

Regardless of the content domain, people with learning disabilities generally learn better when the amount to be learned is controlled, the amount of practice is monitored, and reinforcement theory is applied deliberately by the teacher (Lyon and Moats 1988). To build word images in memory and to ensure that words are so well learned that they can be recalled without delay or conscious thought, a great deal of practice of a few elements at a time is required. A good rule of thumb is 80% old information, 20% new information in a lesson plan designed for a person who spells poorly. Fernald (1943) showed that some children required up to 40 opportunities to write a word correctly before they remembered it.

The number of words presented at one time also needs to be limited for poor spellers. Rieth et al. (1974) found that poor spellers recalled words better by the end of the week if they learned five or six a day and were tested on those daily. Good spellers, however, learned well with as many as twenty words given on Monday. Bryant, Drabin, and Gettinger (1981) found that students with severe spelling disabilities did best with only three new words a day. This data is most applicable to situations when students are trying *to memorize specific words.*

When students are being taught a concept, rule, or generalization about sound-symbol correspondence, such as the "f, l, s doubling rule," only one concept or pattern should be taught at a time. However, ample practice with 30 or more examples in one lesson is often necessary for the redundant pattern to be internalized. Children learn patterns through repeated exposure to many examples. Poor spellers need more experience with print and more focus and repetition during that experience than good spellers.

Modeling and immediate feedback

Effective teaching with poor spellers also entails direct teaching and much interaction between student and teacher. Passive activities such as worksheets and telling a student to look over words are ineffective (Graham and Freeman 1986). Teachers will get the best results if they give students immediate corrective feedback when they make errors and if they model active study strategies for students. One strategy that has been validated with students with learning disabilities is error imitation and modeling (Gerber 1986). The teacher reproduces the child's error and then corrects it, highlighting the difference between the incorrect and correct words, before asking the student to write the word correctly. A more informative approach is to cue the student immediately on a principle, pattern, or mnemonic device that has been temporarily forgotten, or to give an exaggerated "spelling pronunciation" by syllables (e.g., *fam-i-ly*).

Multisensory instruction

The term *multisensory* refers to the simultaneous engagement of hearing, seeing, saying, and feeling during spelling practice. The initials VAKT— visual, auditory, kinesthetic, tactile—refer to multisensory instruction. Children might be asked to say a word while writing it with fingers on a rough surface, or might be asked to say a word slowly, analyze its sounds, say the letters that correspond to sounds, and write them, for example. Although it is not entirely clear from research why multisensory techniques are most efficacious with dyslexic children, experienced remedial teachers have recommended them for decades (e.g., Fernald 1943; Gillingham and Stillman 1960; King 1984) and they have been shown experimentally to produce better results than unisensory techniques with naive or dyslexic children (Bradley 1981; Bryant and Bradley 1985; Hulme, Monk, and Ives 1987; Thomson 1991).

One likely reason for the efficacy of the multisensory approach is that it encourages the child to externalize and focus upon the phonemic elements of the word by saying it slowly and deliberately, noticing how each phoneme is represented. This activity facilitates the "comparator function" viewed as central to spelling by Lindamood, Bell, and Lindamood (1992), the active differentiation of similar word forms and conscious matching of sound to symbol. Moreover, more attention is deployed when several sensory modalities are engaged simultaneously, probably resulting in increased brain activation levels and increased chances for information storage.

Organized and sequential instruction

Children who are poor spellers are insensitive to the structure of spoken and written language and they need much more practice than good spellers to remember sound-symbol associations. They do not spontaneously perceive the semantic, phonological, or orthographic relationships among words derived from one another. When the correspondences, syllable patterns, or other redundancies of the language are presented one at a time in a logical sequence, the elements are differentiated, brought into focus, and related to one another. All the elements are not equally difficult, and repetition of the hardest concepts and associations can be built into lessons as needed.

Whether there is an ideal system for teaching the sequence is open to debate. There does, however, seem to be substantial commonality among spelling programs, so that a basic scope and sequence is approximated by most (table 16).

This scope and sequence seems to represent a natural order of word learning that corresponds to phonological development, reading development, and vocabulary acquisition. The use of such a scope and sequence allows for the orderly introduction of redundant elements and the systematic exploration of their relationships.

SEQUENCE OF SPELLING INSTRUCTION

The components of spelling instruction described below follow the general scope and sequence of table 16, but are not intended to be used in a lockstep manner. Teaching should be flexible and recursive. New concepts can be introduced while other concepts are being mastered and automatized through varied practice.

Where to begin and what to emphasize should depend upon the child's instructional level, regardless of chronological age. As discussed previously, children are more likely to learn words well and retain them if they are studying patterns that are not too difficult (Invernizzi, Abouzeid, and Gill 1994; Morris et al. in press). Not only can the Qualitative Inventory of Spelling Development be a helpful guide to identifying instructional level, but children's spelling attempts will indicate whether they are ready to learn a given word pattern. If they are experimenting with a sound-symbol correspondence or orthographic pattern ("using and confusing" it) they are probably ready for formal instruction in that pattern. A tentative matching of spelling level, reading level, and instructional strategies for beginning students is presented in table 17.[2]

Explicit Practice with Phonemic Analysis

Because spelling is facilitated by an internal representation of a word's phonemic structure, phonemic awareness activities should be incorporated

---

[2]This proposed sequence represents incorporation of ideas from Invernizzi, Abouzeid, and Gill 1994, other unpublished papers of Mary Abouzeid, and the author's viewpoint.

TABLE 16 SPELLING SCOPE AND SEQUENCE CHART

Grade Level	1	2	3	4	5	6	7	8
Beginning Consonants	b c d f g h j k l m n p r s t v w y z		qu	c:cent g:gent				
Ending Consonants	b d g m n p t	x ff ll ss zz			ck-k ge-dge			
Beginning Blends		bl cl fl gl pl sl br cr dr fr gr pr tr sc sk sl sm sn sp st sw	scr spr spl str squ	shr thr		sch		
Ending Blends		mp nd ft lt nt lf st nk ng						
Digraphs		ch sh th	wh-	ph	ch tch	ch:ache chorus		
Silent Letters			ck lk	wr kn	gn			
Vowels	short a c i o u	long a-e e-e i-e o-e u-e	y as long i: sky	y as long e: happy		ie ei schwa (ə)	y as short i: system eigh augh ough	
Vowel Digraphs		ai ee oa ea	au aw oo: boot ew	oo: foot				
Diphthongs			ou ow oi oy					
r-control			ar er ir or ur	air ear				
Prefixes				ur- re-	pre- en- dis- mis- ex- in	con- per- com- a-	bi- mal- circum-inter intra- super- trans	Derivational doubling: immature irregular
Grammatical Endings		No base change -s -ed -ing	Double final consonant Drop final e	Change y to i - ed -ing -er -est			Double final consonant of accepted syllable: regretted	
Suffixes				-ly -ful- -ness -less	-tion -sion -teen	-ment -en	Adjective suffixes: -our -able -ible -ic -al	Noun suffixes: tion -sion -al -ment -ian -ance -ence -tious -cial -ture
Syllables: open and closed		Concept of syllable	Divide compound words sail / boat	Divide Words with prefixes and suffixes: re / turn sad / ly	Divide cvc words: mo/ment Divide vccv words: trum / pet	Suffix -le takes preceding consonant: ta / ble	Vowel digraphs and dipthongs remain undivided in syllables: com / pound	
Contractions			I'm he's she's it's	'll: he'll n't: aren't	'd: we'd 're: you're 've: they've			
Sample Words	lap run flop yet big	sniff stamp chops made load	quitting striding why snoop smart	rice shrilly unhook hurried phone	gnat prediction token napkin judge	school receive neither noble compartment	submitting humorous destructive horizontal agreeable	accord funeral version librarian spatial

L.C. Moats, in collaboration with G. Giveans and teachers from Dresden School District, Hanover, New Hampshire.

TABLE 17. MATCHING SPELLING AND READING ACTIVITIES TO STAGE OF LITERACY DEVELOPMENT.

EMERGENT LITERACY

Knows	*Needs to Learn*	*Strategies*
1. a few alphabet letters	all alphabet letters	alphabet naming, writing, matching
2. clapping syllables	phoneme awareness	Say It and Move It; phoneme counting
3. writes his or her name	letter-sound match	picture matching by beginning sound
		draw pictures and label
		make personal ABC book
4. sense of story	concept of word	reading picture/sign captions
		choral and echo reading
		finger point reading of predictable books
	30–50 sight words	build word bank on cards
	retell a story	video or audio recording of retelling
		make a book in pictures and retell

PHONETIC SPELLING STAGE

1. basic sight vocabulary	100 to 150 words	build word bank in file box
2. preprimer reading	oral reading in pattern books	repeated reading of simple, short books
		taped oral reading, 90% accuracy
3. consonant cues for decoding new words	use vowel and consonant cues to decode	word sorting by vowel/consonant families
		memorize vowel circle
		match vowels in words to vowel circle
4. spell whole words phonetically	use correct short vowel, blends	word building with blocks/letter tiles
5. attempts to write sentences	complete sentences	write to dictation
		compose complete sentences with visual structure
	discriminate sentence types	identify questions, statements
		partner, journal, caption writing
6. listening comprehension	formal text comprehension	graphic representation or meaning
		directed listening-thinking activity
		story prediction, oral summaries

BEGINNING TO MID-FIRST GRADE LEVEL

1. most short vowels, blends, digraphs	long vowel patterns	word sorting; word building with cards; reading nonsense words out of context
2. word by word reading	increase fluency	partner reading, timed repeated reading, taped reading at instructional level
3. sight vocabary + 100	speed of pattern recognition	speed drills
		increase sight word bank
4. uses context to make sense of words	comprehension of reference, word meaning, sentences	sentence linking, graphic organizers
		directed reading-thinking activity
		thematic vocabulary study
5. writes without plan	plan before writing	graphic organizers, categorizing ideas
		publish own books

into spelling lessons for children who have difficulty representing words phonetically. Awareness can be developed through a variety of games and activities that are brief, fun, and interspersed with activities throughout the day.

Introductory phoneme awareness activities.
a) Create silly words, such as names for puppets, animals, and characters,
   using rhyme and alliteration (Bino the Rhino).
b) Point out that known names begin with certain sounds.
c) Contrast words that differ only in one sound (goal—gold).
d) Have children purchase store items or play guessing games by saying
   a"little bit" of a word or getting ready to say a word and producing the
   first sound only.
e) Select a target sound for the day, and praise the student for
   recognizing when the sound occurs in names.

More explicit forms of word analysis.
a) Identify initial phonemes in words through analysis of rhymes. Using
   blocks or chips, show children how a rhyme is formed by changing the
   initial phoneme. Say, "Your name is Jason. Now, if I take off the /j/ and
   add an /m/, I can make a rhyme—Mason! Now you try it.
b) Identify an initial phoneme in words while moving a block or chip.
   Use continuant phonemes (/f/, /s/, /m/, /n/, /l/, /r/, /th/, /v/, /z/) rather
   than stops because it is easier to emphasize and elongate a continuant
   than a stop.
c) Identify the phonemes in a consonant-vowel combination
   (Sue, moo, new, shoe), moving a block for each sound and blending the
   sounds together. Then change the vowel and show with the blocks
   what happened (Sue, see, say, so).
d) Add a final consonant to consonant-vowel combinations and represent
   each phoneme with a block (su + p = sup).
e) Use Ball and Blachman's (1991) "Say It and Move It" procedure: The
   child is presented with a line drawing of an object he/she can name.
   Below the picture is a rectangle divided into sections that correspond
   to the number of phonemes in a word. The teacher models, then the
   child puts a chip in a section as he/she says the word slowly. Then the
   child says the blended word fast. After playing this game with many
   different words, the child can be given chips of different colors to represent the consonants and the vowels. Later, letter tiles can be substituted for chips and beginning spelling can occur. (Ambiguous vowels,
   diphthongs, r-controlled vowels, and consonant blends should be
   avoided at this stage). Beginning awareness of inflections such as plural
   /s/ can also be developed at this stage.

f) Play sound-deletion games after Rosner's (1973) auditory analysis activities:
1. syllable deletion from a compound (say "sunshine" without the "sun")
2. syllable deletion (say "cucumber" without the "cu")
3. initial consonant deletion ("part"without the /p/)
4. final consonant deletion ("seat" without the /t/)
5. initial phoneme in a blend ("stake" without the /s/)
6. final phoneme in a blend ("past" without the /t/)
7. second consonant in an initial blend ("stake" without the /t/)

g) Coding with colored blocks (after *Auditory Discrimination in Depth,* Lindamood and Lindamood 1975): The child uses colored blocks to represent sounds and shows changes where they occur in spoken syllables by changing the color of a block, adding a block, or taking a block away. If sounds are the same, the same color should represent them; if sounds are different, different colors should be used. An order for level of difficulty is as follows:
1. add a sound (if this says /i/, show me /ip/)
2. delete a sound (if this says /kap/, show me /ap/)
3. change a consonant (if this says /slap/ show me /snap/)
4. change a vowel: (if this says /slap/, show me /slop/)
5. change the order of sounds (pats to past)
6. duplicate a sound already in the word (art to tart)

Once skill is developed with colored blocks, then letter tiles can be gradually substituted for them.

Additional phonological awareness activities suitable for older students:
a) With one-syllable words, have the student say each word slowly, separating the phonemes, and marking each sound on a finger. Model this for the student as often as necessary.
b) Given an array of counters that correspond to the phonemes in longer words such as *silver,* ask the student which one corresponds to /l/ or some other sound.
c) If the student has difficulty representing a vowel, be sure he or she has identified the vowel in the syllable correctly by saying it in isolation and giving a cue word beginning with the vowel.
d) Deliberately contrast prefixes and words that have subtle differences in pronunciation, such as *pre, per*, and *pro; migrate* and *migraine,* by dictating these slowly and having the student spell them with letter tiles.
e) Words in a student's writing vocabulary can be categorized by sound. For example, awareness of confusable blends such as *fr* and *fl* can be enhanced by grouping words such as *flagrant* and *fragrant* with others beginning with the same clusters.

Teaching Basic Sound-Symbol Correspondences

The most basic multisensory drill advocated by Gillingham and Stillman (1960) and other programs based on similar principles (Clark 1988) includes viewing a letter form on a card, saying the letter name, saying a key word, and then saying the target phoneme in isolation ("i, itchy, /I/") The letter form is traced on a rough surface as the student recites. To spell, the order of drill is changed to saying the sound, the key word, and the letter that makes it, and then writing the letter. The Orton-Gillingham approach seeks automatic learning of these associations, and even after longer words are being spelled successfully, the student is asked to repeat the drill at the beginning of each lesson. As associations are learned, words are spelled using the Gillingham Simultaneous Oral Spelling (S.O.S.) technique (Gillingham and Stillman 1960), to establish reliance on a phonetic encoding strategy:

1) The teacher pronounces the word.
2) The child hears the word and repeats the word. (He is hearing his own voice and feeling the articulation.)
3) The child says the word sound by sound; after identifying each phoneme, he says the name of the letter that represents the sound, and writes the letter as it is being named.
4) The child reads back the word he has written orally.

Many older children are not sure of all the alphabet letter names or forms even though they have been in school for several years. Some of the most confusable letters are *u*, *y*, and *w*, because their names, sounds, and forms relate in misleading ways to one another. For example, the letter name "y" begins with a /w/, the sound represented by *w*. Letters at the end of the alphabet are often learned less well than those at the beginning because less time is spent practicing them and fewer words use them (u, v, w, x, y, z). Often, the alphabet names and forms must be retaught to remedial students.

Choice of an unambiguous key word containing each phoneme is critically important in the basic sound-symbol drill. Desirable key words to associate with the short vowel phonemes, for example, would avoid nasalized vowels, r-controlled vowels, or vowels that are distorted by the following consonant. Suggested key words are as follows:

Vowel	*Key Word*	*Words to Avoid*
/æ/	at, apple	ant, bag, air
/ɛ/	Ed, Eddy	egg, elephant
/ɪ/	it, icky	igloo, Indian, ink

| /a/ | ox, octopus | on, off |
| /ʌ/ | up, us | umbrella, uncle |

If students have severe difficulties with phoneme identification, the Auditory Discrimination in Depth Program of Lindamood and Lindamood (1975) is recommended for teaching sound-symbol correspondence. An emphasis on articulatory feedback to develop phonemic awareness for reading and spelling has been validated for children with severe phonological processing deficits and severe reading handicaps (Alexander et al. 1991; Howard 1982; Torgesen and Morgan 1992). In this program, children are first taught to identify the speech sounds of English by their place and manner of articulation. For example, the voiced/voiceless contrasts of eight consonant pairs are taught directly before symbols for the phonemes are introduced, and the articulatory positions of /l/ and /r/ are taught to aid their discrimination. Vowels are contrasted by position in the mouth.

A practice of the Lindamood and Gillingham approaches that should be incorporated into any remedial spelling program is the explicit and correct definition of linguistic concepts. Vowels are a set of speech sounds; digraphs are different from blends; schwa is the unaccented vowel, and so forth. Even young children can learn this terminology. It serves to clarify, not confuse, but of course the teacher must be well informed about language to teach these concepts.

Persistent letter confusions and letter reversals can usually be corrected with a multisensory drill and daily practice reading and writing words with the confusable letters. Immediate corrective feedback must be available at first until the student internalizes a self-checking strategy. Reference to a mnemonic image, such as a *bed* for *b* and *d*, is often helpful, along with an alphabet taped to the writing desk.

Teaching Regular One-Syllable Patterns

The basic units of spelling should be presented and learned in an order progressing from high frequency, high regularity units to complex, more unusual units that operate within several constraints. Forbes (1968), for example, organized her word lists into those that could be "sounded out," those that could be "sounded out and thought out," and those that required memorization or thorough knowledge of complex rules and probabilities. The first level of practice occurs with predictable consonants, short-vowel word families or recurring syllable patterns. Initial presentation of a new pattern should ask the student to actively reorganize, compare, contrast, and sort word lists by their initial consonant(s) and by their rime (Morris 1982; Sulzby 1980). Lists of words sharing rime features should be kept for later reference (e.g., *mass, grass, compass*) and for adding new words as they are encountered. Comparison, sorting, and classification are much more effective than rule recitation alone for learning about patterns, although ample practice writing words will be necessary to reinforce their automatic recall. A sorting of words with various recurring vowel team patterns might look like this:

ee	ie	ea
meet	fiend	peace
sheep	piece	knead
speed	niece	cream

Vowel spellings, again, are the most varied and require the most practice. At first, the single letter and vowel-consonant-e patterns should be taught, then the vowel digraphs and diphthongs, one at a time. Vowels followed by /l/, /r/, and nasals /m/ and /n/ will be the most challenging for students because the presence and identity of the consonant as separate from the vowel is difficult for dyslexic students to realize. These constructions are phonologically ambiguous or obscure. In addition, the spellings in *hurt, bird, learn, were, her,* and *favor* all map to the same indistinct vowel plus /r/, and the word *fire* sounds as if it has two syllables, as in *higher.* Many poor spellers never quite master these complexities, so repeated practice with different patterns should be ongoing even when more advanced multisyllable words are being studied.

Corrective feedback should take into account the reason for a child's confusion about spelling. Very often, the phonological ambiguity of the words themselves will be the cause of a misspelling. For example, if the child spells BAG for *beg,* the student could be taught that the vowel in *beg* is in fact pronounced like a "long a," but that this distortion in speaking is ignored in writing, and the word is to be grouped with the family that includes *leg, keg, Meg,* and *egg.*

Early Introduction of Inflections

As soon as students are reading and writing verb forms, they are ready to be introduced to the past tense *-ed* morpheme. As soon as they are reading and writing noun forms, they are ready to learn the plural /s/ spelling. Learning that these morphemes are spelled consistently in spite of variations in pronunciation is the first step to realizing that spelling represents meaning, often in preference to sound. Explicit teaching of the past tense necessitates identification of the /d/, /t/, or /ed/ that ends words such as *begged, walked,* and *wanted,* before words are written to dictation. Inflection spellings should be reviewed and practiced often for many years. Do not present one lesson on each and expect the learning to be internalized.

Conditional Word and Syllable Patterns

Many patterns and generalizations are predictable but conditional. They include the spellings of *tall, annoy, glue, glove,* and *most.* In these cases, the student can either be asked to understand a pattern from examples (inductive learning) or to apply a given rule or principle to examples (deductive learning). The inductive approach is a powerful tool with bright students who enjoy solving puzzles. It is illustrated by the following exercise to teach the ch, tch generalization:

Given this list of words,

inch	catch	bunch	kitchen
starch	pouch	fetch	butcher
pitch	march	ranch	pinch
hatchet	pooch	botch	stitch

ask students to state when tch is used to spell /č/ at the ends of words or syllables. Students may realize there are a few exceptions, including *rich, much, such, which, attach, sandwich,* and *bachelor,* and these should be presented as atypical. The word sort activity, helpful for discovering principles, can be carried out with words given on cards or with lists of words that the student generates.

If the deductive approach is confusing or ineffective with students because they are unable to see the patterns in the examples, then a deductive approach might be taken. A deductive approach calls for the teacher to state the rule and ask the student(s) to apply it to examples. With the word list above, the teacher might state, "A one-syllable word ending in /č/ spells it tch after an accented short vowel. In all other cases, /č/ is spelled ch." Then words could be grouped, read, and spelled to dictation.

Homophones

Their, there, and *they're; you're* and *your; its* and *it's* are among the most often misspelled words in the language. Other spellings of words that sound the same but differ in meaning and spelling, such as *course* and *coarse, knight* and *night, prophet* and *profit* are commonly confused by children who cannot rely on letter memory. The best one can hope for in cases of very poor spellers is to clarify confusions among words they use most often, because practice in context is what eventually develops the correct word habit.

Teachers often claim it takes an entire year of repeated practice to straighten out the *there/there/they're* confusion in older children who learned these words incorrectly. Matching games in which spelling and meaning are paired are helpful, at least in sensitizing the writer to what must be looked up, along with dictated phrases given regularly. Spell checkers on computers do not catch such errors and they can be embarrassing (like the letter from the ski coach who asked parents to learn the *coarse* before *gait*-keeping). A comprehensive list of homophones can be found in *Spellmaster* (Greebaum

1987); another is published in the *New Reading Teacher's Book of Lists* (Fry, Fountoukidis, and Polk 1985). Recall is facilitated when the words are placed in meaningful contexts repeatedly, including phrases, sentences, cloze exercises, analogies, jokes, cartoons, and puns. Homophones should be taught a few at a time; however, only the most able learners can work with the long lists that often appear in workbooks.

Syllable Patterns and Syllable Juncture

The syllable should be defined as a pronounceable unit that always contains a vowel sound and vowel letter (exceptions *rhythm; -ism*). Children with spelling difficulties benefit from learning the six syllable types (table 5, Chapter 1). One reason for teaching syllables is that redundant patterns in longer words can be much more quickly discerned; another is that the rules for adding endings to words and the way in which syllables are combined into longer words depend on the type of syllable(s) in the word; and finally, spellings become more predictable when the type of syllable is taken into account. For example, the most common spelling of "long a" in an open syllable within a multisyllable word (*radio, vacation, stable*) is simply the letter a, and not the other seven alternatives.

If one knows about syllable types, one can remember more easily that *accommodate* has two *m's:* because the second vowel is short it most likely is followed by two consonants, one ending the closed "com" syllable, the other beginning the open "mo" syllable. The word *little* has two *t's* because the first syllable is closed and the last syllable is a standard consonant-le configuration. A double *n* is necessary in words like *beginning* because the second syllable is closed and double letter protects the "short i" vowel sound. There are many excellent programs for teaching syllable structure, including the *Brody Reading Method* (Brody 1987), *Words* (Henry 1990), *Megawords* (Johnson and Bayrd 1983), *Solving Language Difficulties* (Steere, Peck and Kahn 1971), and the game *Syllable Plus* (Stoner 1985).

Latin and Greek Morpheme Patterns

Latin-based words are usually taught after basic Anglo-Saxon vocabulary has been learned (Henry 1993). In some ways they are easier to spell than Anglo-Saxon words. They do not use the problematic digraphs so common in Anglo-Saxon spellings, and because many spellings are meaning-based prefixes, roots, and suffixes, they tend to be constant even though many are reduced to /ə/ when they are unaccented. If students learn to recognize those meaningful units, many spellings will seem more logical. For example, *recommend* would not have two *c's*, because the prefix *re* is added to the root *commend*.

There is ample evidence from cognitive psychology that words sharing derivational relationships should be taught together to older students (Moats and Smith 1992; Templeton 1992). Many roots of Latin origin have consonants whose phonetic form changes in derived words such as the t, c, and s that appear in *partial; magician; confusion.* In addition, reduced vowels can be ambiguous in various derived forms (*confidence; sedative; competition*). In many words with ambiguous vowels or chameleon consonants, the correct spelling of a base word or derivation can be recovered more easily if it is learned in partnership with a word sharing the same root and more transparent pronunciation (Henry 1993; Hodges 1981; Templeton 1992). On any list of "hard to spell" words, there are some that can be taught so that root-derivative relationships are explicated: *differ, different; favor, favorite; child, children; autumn, autumnal; sign, signal, resign, resignation; vacate, vacation; athlete, athletic; theater, theatrical; magic, magician.*

Many other words that turn up on "hard to spell" lists are rule-based or comprise affix-root constructions that help make sense of the spelling . There is no reason *beneficial, advice, attend,* or *misspell* should be learned in isolation as sight words, when all have prefixes. The method for teaching such words should call attention to a word's structure at the levels of sound, syllable, and meaningful parts.

Words of Greek origin make up a large segment of our scientific vocabulary, and are best studied in the context of science and math. The spellings of *y* for /I/ (*gym, sphynx, crypton*), *ph* for /f/ (*photo, sphere, graph*) and *ch* for /k/ (*chorus, chameleon, ache*) signify a Greek derivative. Greek words combine morphemes but assign them equal status, like English compounds (*stratosphere, phonograph, thermometer*). The spellings tend to be consistent and phonically transparent, and thus easier than words from other languages. *Words* (Henry, 1990) is a program that emphasizes morphology and word origin.

To illustrate, the word *mnemonic* might seem obscure and difficult to spell until one considers its Greek origin and the related forms that have entered English. Mnemosyne was the Greek goddess of memory. The words *amnesia* (without memory) and *amnesty* (literally, forgetting a transgression) are cousins of *mnemonic.* Such knowledge helps clarify for most people that the other phonetically confusable Greek root, *pneumo* (*pneumatic, pneumonia*) is an altogether different form having to do with air. Memory and air, are, we hope, unrelated entities.

About Ending Rules

The three major rules requiring an orthographic change when endings are added to words seem daunting for students to learn and frustrating for teachers to teach (see table 6, Chapter 1). The only hope for teaching these rules is to present them at intervals over several years, along with repeated reinforcement when corrective feedback about spelling is given. Consistent practice is needed rather than one or two lessons in sixth grade. Furthermore, these rules should be introduced after students have the conceptual underpinnings: a firm grasp of single-syllable spellings; the concepts of consonant, vowel, and syllable; and the ability to read multiple examples.

Most people begin to internalize the patterns for spelling word endings through repeated exposure to them in print. A good speller can produce a rule-based construction without necessarily stating the rule accurately, although knowledge of the rules helps clarify what is right when specific word memory fails. Individuals with mild spelling difficulties profit from practice with rules because their attention can be focused on the entire letter sequence in words such as *beginning* and *easier* when the spelling makes sense.

The internalization of orthographic change rules is very difficult for many poor spellers. Often students with spelling disability will fail to recognize when a rule needs to be applied, even if they know the rule (Carlisle 1987; Liberman et al. 1985). Spelling research suggests that poor spellers will often recall specific word spellings without evidence that they have internalized or automated the rule that governs them.

INSTRUCTIONAL STRATEGIES ACROSS THE SEQUENCE
Memorizing Words as Wholes

Multisensory techniques can be applied to the memorization of individual words. Even Horn (1969), who was generally hostile to linguistic or rule-based spelling instruction, notes that word study was more effective when several sensory images were stimulated simultaneously. His word study method follows:

1. look at the word,
2. pronounce the word,
3. say the letter names,
4. recall how the word looks with the eyes closed,
5. look back at the word and check,
6. write the word, and
7. check and repeat if necessary.

This particular method, however, avoids explicit analysis of speech sounds and their representations. The Fitzgerald method (Fitzgerald 1951) places more emphasis on linking meaning with spelling, and remains an effective multisensory technique for memorizing words with somewhat unpredictable or complex spelling patterns:

1. *Meaning and pronunciation.* Have the child look at the word, pronounce it, and use it in a sentence.
2. *Imagery.* Ask the child to see the word and say the word. Have the child say the word by syllable, spell the word orally, and trace over the word with a finger or write it in the air.
3. *Recall.* Ask the child to look at the word and then close her eyes to see the word in her mind's eye. Have her spell the word orally with her eyes closed. Ask her to open her eyes and see if the spelling was correct.
4. *Write the word.* The child writes the word from memory, and then checks against the original.
5. *Mastery.* The child covers the word and writes it. If she is correct, she should cover it and write it two more times.

The Fernald (1943) technique is similar to the above, but the whole word is traced repeatedly with the index and middle fingers on a rough tactile surface until the child can write it from memory. The learned word is then placed in the context of a meaningful sentence. There is no concern for grouping words by phonic pattern in Fernald's approach.

Such techniques foster the recall of specific images for words that a student must commit to memory. They should accompany explicit instruction in the patterns and logic of the spelling system, which, if learned, will facilitate the whole word learning process. There is some evidence (Vaughn, Schumm, and Gordon 1993) that a variety of motoric conditions can be used for multisensory practice of spelling words, including writing, tracing, or typing on a computer, and each of these is equally beneficial.

Promoting the Use of Active Recall Strategies

Although many programs offer suggestions for mnemonic devices that will aid spelling recall, the most effective mnemonics are those that students make up themselves. Because more active mental processing is necessary to create an idea than to listen to one, the self-generated strategy is the one most likely to be used. Children's word recall can be enhanced if they are taught to identify the words they are unsure of and to write plausible alternatives (Nulman and Gerber 1984).

Planned Generalization of Skill

Most children who spell poorly can learn some words in lists with sufficient practice, but regress to old habits during spontaneous writing. Instruction is not worthwhile unless it generalizes. Regular dictation exercises, personal spelling dictionaries with words listed alphabetically, typing words on the computer, and proofreading practice can strengthen the bridge between spelling skill development and its automatic use. Furthermore, overlearning basic sound-symbol associations and syllable patterns, and rehearsing words using multisensory drills prior to writing them in text facilitates generalization.

Brody (1987), for example, suggests that informal classroom use of syllabication and multiple word writing improves spelling. Her steps include:

1. Student says words in syllables.
2. Student writes word with spaces between syllables while subvocalizing pronunciation of each syllable (no line or slash between syllables).
3. Student writes word as whole.
4. Words are written repeatedly, 5 times each, in syllables, over 3-5 days.

Integrated Lesson Planning

A systematic teacher plans the major elements of a lesson according to a predefined sequence of skills, and keeps an informal record of a student's responses to instruction. Although the plan can always be adjusted, it serves as a guide by which good teaching principles are implemented. Such a plan includes a choice of appropriate examples, sufficient review and practice, and application of skills to meaningful writing. On the basis of detailed record keeping, the next lesson can be tailor-made. *Spellmaster* (Greenbaum 1987) is a system for individualizing instruction for a class group. An individual progress record and data sheet for recording the specific spelling patterns each student has mastered accompany a detailed set of word lists and instructional activities.

Systematic spelling instruction usually occurs in coordination with reading and vocabulary instruction. A remedial lesson plan within a multisensory, linguistic approach might be similar to this:

1. phonogram drill
    a) sound-symbol
    b) symbol-sound
2. writing syllables and/or words to dictation; immediate correction of errors by reference to logic or known words; review of previously learned material
3. sight word practice using multisensory writing-saying technique
4. introduction of new concept using inductive method or deductive method, as appropriate; exploration of phonological, orthographic, and etymological facts about the concept

5. locating instances of new concept in text; sorting and matching activity
6. sentence writing activity using new words

Individual Differences and Flexible Teaching

Various strategies work for different types of words and different types of children. All of the specific suggestions offered here are useful at some point with some children. For example, brighter children need quick integration of basic patterns into advanced vocabulary (*patch, dispatch, dispatcher; cent, century, percent, centennial*), but slower children might be overwhelmed by exposure to the harder words or words not in their speaking vocabulary. It is essential to have available a comprehensive word list that includes examples of each sound-symbol correspondence, syllable type, spelling pattern, rule, or generalization (e.g., Forbes 1968; Greenbaum 1987; Henderson 1990) and to use it with flexibility.

As Stanback (1980) concluded after reviewing the historical literature on teaching spelling, there is no one right way to represent word structure for children or to help them remember this information. Techniques for making word structure memorable should vary according to the words under study. These strategies should match the properties of the target word presented as well as the learner's capabilities (Schlagal and Schlagal 1992).

Additional Strategies to Aid Memorization

Several additional strategies for spelling instruction can be helpful when employed selectively and sensibly:

1. *Invoke a "spelling pronunciation".* This works well for words with silent letters, and foreign or irregular spellings that do not match pronunciation, such as *Wednesday, was,* and *antique.*
2. *Group words with like, but unusual, spelling-meaning patterns.*

two	one	there	their
twenty	once	here	heir
twelve	only	where	

3. *Employ mnemonic devices (association links):*
He **meant** to be **mean**. There's **a rat** in sep**arat**e. Knights would **die val**iantly in me**dieval** times. **Loose** as a **goose.** It's hard to **lose** your **nose. Sally** fin**all**y came home.

4. *Highlight visual-orthographic features of words.* People with poor orthographic memory may store and retrieve word images more read-

ily if novelty or contrast is used to highlight letter sequences. Techniques that may be useful include: color coding (to contrast vowels and consonants); underlining; using different fonts on a word processor; or writing letters in different sizes. The effectiveness of such manipulations is not well researched at present, however.

Special Considerations for Teaching Adolescents

Adolescents and adults often view themselves as hopeless cases if they have spelling disabilities, especially if prior instruction has been haphazard or linguistically uninformed. Many of them, however, can make significant improvement if their disabilities are addressed systematically, sequentially, and logically over a sustained period of time. When instruction is aimed at their developmental level of word knowledge, they can develop confidence that language makes sense and that many spelling problems can be solved with knowledge of language structure. They often know many individual words but do not understand spelling principles or word relationships. Adolescents have a much larger oral vocabulary to draw upon, so that rimes and other syllable units can be immediately applied to many examples. Their vocabulary can be used to build understanding of redundant language patterns.

Goals for accuracy must be modest and realistic. Instruction should be aimed at improving the person's chances to communicate clearly and recognize the need to check a spelling.

A FINAL WORD

The teacher of spelling who knows our language intimately can clarify the patterns of English for the learner. When a teacher understands the course of spelling development and meaning of various error patterns, the level of instruction can be matched to each student. Individual variation in spelling is extremely wide in any classroom, and a knowledgeable teacher is able to survey the developmental levels of the students and provide meaningful practice at those levels. The design of effective instruction and practice will depend upon the nature of the vocabulary to be learned, the developmental level of the learner, and the presence of any learning disability. Successful teaching will net more than improved spelling; it will also strengthen the learner's appreciation of language and result in more proficient decoding skills. Learning to spell necessitates becoming familiar with our language, including its history, structure, and meaning. What more essential subject could there be.

References

Adams, M. 1990. *Beginning to Read: Thinking and Learning About Print*. Cambridge, MA: MIT Press.

Alexander, A. W., Andersen, H. G., Heilman, P. C., Voeller, K. S., and Torgesen, J. K. 1991. Phonological awareness training and remediation of analytic decoding deficits in a group of severe dyslexics. *Annals of Dyslexia* 41:193–206.

Bailet, L. L. 1990. Spelling rule usage among students with learning disabilities and normally achieving students. *Journal of Learning Disabilities* 23:121–28.

Bailet, L. L., and Lyon, G. R. 1985. Deficient linguistic rule application in a learning disabled speller: A case study. *Journal of Learning Disabilities* 18:162–65.

Bain, A. M., Bailet, L. L., and Moats, L. C., eds. 1991. *Written Language Disorders: Theory into Practice*. Austin, TX: PRO-ED.

Ball, E. W. 1993. Phonological awareness: What's important and to whom? *Reading and Writing: An Interdisciplinary Journal* 5:141–59.

Ball, E. W., and Blachman, B. A. 1991. Does phoneme awareness training in kindergarten make a difference in early word recognition and spelling development? *Reading Research Quarterly* 26:46–66.

Balmuth, M. 1992. *The Roots of Phonics*. Baltimore: York Press.

Baron, J., and Treiman, R. 1980. Use of orthography in reading and learning to read. In *Orthography, Reading, and Dyslexia*, eds. J. F. Kavanagh and R. L. Venezky. Baltimore: University Park Press.

Bear, D. R. 1992. The prosody of oral reading and stages of word knowledge. In *Development of Orthographic Knowledge and the Foundations of Literacy*, eds. S. Templeton and D. R. Bear. Hillsdale, NJ: Lawrence Erlbaum.

Beers, J. 1980. Developmental strategies of spelling competence in primary school children. In *Developmental and Cognitive Aspects of Learning to Spell: A Reflection of Word Knowledge*, eds. E. Henderson and J. Beers. Newark, DE: International Reading Association.

Beers, J., and Henderson, E. 1977. A study of developing orthographic concepts among first graders. *Research in the Teaching of English* 11:133–48.

Beers, C. S., and Beers, J. W. 1992. Children's spelling of English inflectional morphology. In *Development of Orthographic Knowledge and the Foundations of Literacy*, eds. S. Templeton and D. R. Bear. Hillsdale, NJ: Lawrence Erlbaum.

Berninger, V. C., Yates, A., Cartwright, J., Rutberg, E., Remy, and Abbott, R. 1992. Lower-level developmental skills in beginning writing. *Reading and Writing: An Interdisciplinary Journal* 4:257–80.

109

Bissex, G. 1980. *Gnys at Wrk: A Child Learns to Write and Read.* Cambridge, MA: Harvard University Press.

Bodecker, J. W., Hillis, A., and Caramazza, A. 1990. Lexical morphology and its role in the writing process: Evidence from a case of acquired dysgraphia. *Cognition* 35: 205–43.

Boder, E. 1973. Developmental dyslexia: A developmental approach based on three atypical reading-spelling patterns. *Developmental Medicine and Child Neurology* 15:663–87.

Boder, E., and Jarrico, S. 1982. *The Boder Test of Reading-Spelling Patterns: A Diagnostic Screening Test for Subtypes of Reading Disability.* Orlando, FL: Grune and Stratton.

Bradley, L. 1981. The organization of motor patterns for spelling: An effective remedial strategy for backward readers. *Developmental Medicine and Child Neurology* 15:663–87.

Bradley, L., and Bryant, P. E. 1983. Categorising sounds and learning to read: A causal connection. *Nature* 310:419–21.

Bradley-Johnson, S., and Lesiak, J. L. 1989. *Problems in Written Expression: Assessment and Remediation.* New York: Guilford.

Brody, S. 1987. *The Brody Reading Manual: An Implementation Guide for Teachers.* Milford, NH: LARC Publishing.

Bruck, M. 1987. The adult outcomes of children with learning disabilities. *Annals of Dyslexia* 37: 252–63.

Bruck, M. 1988. The word recognition and spelling of dyslexic children. *Reading Research Quarterly* 23:51–69.

Bruck, M., and Waters, G. 1988. An analysis of the spelling errors of children who differ in their reading and spelling skills. *Applied Psycholinguistics* 9:77–92.

Bryant, N. D., Drabin, I. R., and Gettinger, M. 1981. Effects of varying unit size on spelling achievement in learning disabled children. *Journal of Learning Disabilities* 14: 200–203.

Bryant, P. E., and Bradley, L. 1985. *Children's Reading Problems.* Oxford: Blackwell.

Bryant, P. E., and Impey, L. 1986. The similarities between normal readers and developmental and acquired dyslexics. *Cognition* 24:121–37.

Bryson, B. 1990. *The Mother Tongue: English and How It Got That Way.* New York: Avon.

Caramazza, A., Miceli, G., Villa, G., and Roman, C. 1987. The role of the graphemic buffer in spelling: Evidence from a case of acquired dysgraphia. *Cognition* 26:59–85.

Carlisle, J. F. 1987. The use of morphological knowledge in spelling derived forms by learning-disabled and normal students. *Annals of Dyslexia* 37:90–108.

Chomsky, C. 1970. Reading, spelling, and phonology. *Harvard Educational Review* 40:287–309.

Chomsky, C. 1979. Approaching reading through invented spelling. In *Theory and Practice of Early Reading,*Vol.2, ed. L. B. Resnick and P. A. Weaver. Hillsdale, NJ: Lawrence Erlbaum.

Chomsky, N., and Halle, M. 1968. *The Sound Pattern of English.* New York: Harper and Row.

Clark, D. B. 1988. *Dyslexia: Theory and Practice of Remedial Instruction.* Parkton, MD: York Press.

Conoley, J. C., and Kramer, J. J. 1989. *The Tenth Mental Measurements Yearbook.* Lincoln, NB: University of Nebraska Press.

Cook, L. 1981. Misspelling analysis in dyslexia: Observation of developmental strategy shifts. *Bulletin of The Orton Dyslexia Society* 31:123–134.

Corcos, E., and Willows, D. M. 1993. The processing of orthographic information. In *Visual Processes in Reading and Reading Disabilities*, eds. D. M. Willows, R. S. Kruk, and E. Corcos. Hillsdale, NJ: Lawrence Erlbaum.

Deno, S. L., Marston, D., and Mirkin, P. K. 1982. Valid measurement procedures for continuous evaluation of written expression. *Exceptional Children* 48:368–71.

Ehri, L. C. 1984. How orthography alters spoken language competencies in children learning to read and spell. In *Language Awareness and Learning to Read*, eds. J. Downing and R. Valtin. New York: Springer-Verlag.

Ehri, L. C. 1986. Sources of difficulty in learning to spell and read. In *Advances in Developmental and Behavioral Pediatrics*, Vol. 7, eds. M. L. Wolraich and D. Routh. Greenwich, CT: JAI press.

Ehri, L. C. 1987. Learning to read and spell words. *Journal of Reading Behavior* 19:5–31.

Ehri, L. C. 1989. The development of spelling knowledge and its role in reading acquisition and reading disability. *Journal of Learning Disabilities* 22:349–64.

Ehri, L. C. 1992. Review and commentary: Stages of spelling development. In *Development of Orthographic Knowledge and the Foundations of Literacy*, eds. S. Templeton and D. R. Bear. Hillsdale, NJ: Lawrence Erlbaum.

Ehri, L. C. 1994. Development of the ability to read words: Update. In *Theoretical Models and Processes of Reading*, eds. R. Ruddell, M. Ruddell, and H. Singer. Newark, DE: International Reading Association.

Ehri, L. C., and Robbins, C. 1992. Beginners need some decoding skill to read words by analogy. *Reading Research Quarterly* 27:13–26.

Ehri, L. C., and Wilce, L. S. 1987. Does learning to spell help beginners learn to read words? *Reading Research Quarterly* 12:47–65.

Ehri, L. C., Wilce, L. S., and Taylor, B. B. 1987. Children's categorization of short vowels in words and the influence of spellings. *Merrill Palmer Quarterly* 33:393–421.

Ellis, A. W. 1993. *Reading, Writing, and Dyslexia: A Cognitive Analysis*, 2nd ed. Hove, UK: Lawrence Erlbaum.

Felton, R. H., and Wood, F. B. 1989. Cognitive deficits in reading disability and attention deficit disorder. *Journal of Learning Disabilities* 1·3–13.

Fernald, G. 1943. *Remedial Techniques in Basic School Subjects*. New York: McGraw Hill.

Fitzgerald, J. A. 1951. *A Basic Life Spelling Vocabulary*. Bruce.

Finucci, J., Gottfredson, L. S., and Childs, B. 1985. A follow-up study of dyslexic boys. *Annals of Dyslexia* 35:117–36.

Finucci, J. M., Isaacs, S. D., Whitehouse, C. C., and Childs, B. 1983. Classification of spelling errors and their relationship to reading ability, sex, grade placement, and intelligence. *Brain and Language* 20:340–55.

Fischer, F. W., Shankweiler, D., and Liberman, I. Y. 1985. Spelling proficiency and sensitivity to word structure. *Journal of Memory and Language* 24:423–41.

Fitzsimmons, R. J., and Loomer, B. M. 1977. *Excerpts from Spelling: Learning and Instruction—Research and Practice*. Iowa City: Iowa State Department of Public Instruction and the University of Iowa.

Flynn, J. M., Deering, W., Goldstein, M., and Rahbar, M. H. 1992. Electrophysiological correlates of dyslexic subtypes. *Journal of Learning Disabilities* 25:133–41.

Foorman, B. R., and Francis, D. J. 1994. Exploring the connections among reading, spelling, and phonemic segmentation during first grade. *Reading and Writing: An Interdisciplinary Journal* 6:65–91.

Forbes, C. T. 1968. *Graded and Classified Spelling Lists for Teachers Grades 2-8.* Cambridge, MA: Educators Publishing Service.

Frauenheim, J. G., and Heckerl, J. R. 1983. A longitudinal study of psychological and achievement test performance in severe dyslexic adults. *Journal of Learning Disabilities* 16:339–47.

Frith, U. 1980a. *Cognitive Processes in Spelling.* New York: Academic Press.

Frith, U. 1980b. Unexpected spelling problems. In *Cognitive Processes in Spelling*, ed. U. Frith. New York: Academic Press.

Frith, U. 1985. Beneath the surface of developmental dyslexia. In *Surface Dyslexia*, eds. K. Patterson, M. Coltheart, and J. Marshall. London: Lawrence Erlbaum.

Frith, U., and Frith, C. 1983. Relationships between reading and spelling. In *Orthography, Reading, and Dyslexia*, eds. J. P. Kavanagh and R. L. Venezky. Baltimore: University Park Press.

Fromkin, V., and Rodman, R. 1984. *An Introduction to Language.* New York: Holt, Rinehart.

Fry, E., Fountoukidis, D. L., and Polk, J. K. 1985. *The New Reading Teacher's Book of Lists.* Englewood Cliffs, NH: Prentice-Hall.

Gentry, J. R. 1978. Early spelling strategies. *The Elementary School Journal* 79:88–92.

Gentry, J. R. 1981. Learning to spell developmentally. *Reading Teacher* 34:378–81.

Gerber, M. 1984. Techniques to teach generalizable spelling skills. *Academic Therapy* 20:49–58.

Gerber, M. 1986. Generalization of spelling strategies by learning disabled students as a result of contingent imitation/modeling and mastery criteria. *Journal of Learning Disabilities* 19: 530–37.

Gerber, M., and Hall, R. 1987. Information processing approaches to studying spelling deficiencies. *Journal of Learning Disabilities* 20:34–42.

Gill, J. T. 1992. The relationship between word recognition and spelling. In *Development of Orthographic Knowledge and the Foundations of Literacy*, eds. S. Templeton and D. R. Bear. Hillsdale, NJ: Lawrence Erlbaum.

Gillingham, A., and Stillman, B. 1960. *Remedial Training for Children with Specific Disability in Reading, Spelling, and Penmanship.* Cambridge, MA: Educators Publishing Service.

Goodman, R., and Caramazza, A. 1986. Dissociation of spelling errors in written and oral spelling: The role of allographic conversion in writing. *Cognitive Neuropsychology* 3:179–206.

Goswami, U. 1988. Orthographic analogies and reading development. *Quarterly Journal of Experimental Psychology* 40:239–68.

Goswami, U. 1992. Annotation: Phonological Factors in Spelling Development. *Journal of Child Psychology and Psychiatry*, 33:967–75.

Goswami, U., and Bryant, P. 1990. *Phonological Skills and Learning to Read.* East Sussex, U.K.: Lawrence Erlbaum.

Graham, S., and Freeman, S. 1986. Strategy training and teacher vs. student controlled study conditions: Effects on learning disabled students' spelling performance. *Learning Disabilities Quarterly* 9:15–22.

Greenbaum, C. R. 1987. *Spellmaster.* Austin, TX: PRO-ED.

Griffith, P. 1991. Phoneme awareness helps first graders invent spellings and third graders remember correct spellings. *Journal of Reading Behavior* 23:215–33.

Grill, J. J., and Kirwin, M. M. 1989. *Written Language Assessment.* Novato, CA: Academic Therapy Publications.

Hammill, D., and Larsen, D. 1987. *Test of Written Language-Revised.* Austin, TX: PRO-ED.

Hanna, P. R., Hanna, J. S., Hodges, R. E., and Rudorf, E. H. 1966. *Phoneme-grapheme Correspondences as Cues to Spelling Improvement.* Washington, DC: U.S. Government Printing Office, U.S. Office of Education.

Hanna, P. R., Hodges, R. E., and Hanna, J. S. 1971. *Spelling: Structure and Strategies.* Boston: Houghton Mifflin.

Henderson, E. 1990. *Teaching Spelling.* Boston: Houghton Mifflin.

Henderson, E. H., and Beers, J. W. eds. 1980. *Developmental and Cognitive Aspects of Learning to Spell: A Reflection of Word Knowledge.* Newark, DE: International Reading Association.

Henry, M. 1988. Beyond phonics: Integrated decoding and spelling instruction based on word origin and structure. *Annals of Dyslexia* 38:258–75.

Henry, M. 1990. *Words.* Los Gatos, CA: Lex Press.

Henry, M. 1993. Morphological structure: Latin and Greek roots and affixes as upper grade code strategies. *Reading and Writing: An Interdisciplinary Journal* 5:227–41.

Hillerich, R. L. 1985. *Teaching Children to Write, K-8: A Complete Guide to Developing Writing Skills.* Englewood Cliffs, NJ: Prentice-Hall.

Hillis, A., and Caramazza, A. 1989. The grapheme buffer and attentional mechanisms. *Brain and Language* 36:208–35.

Hodges, R. E. 1981. *Learning to Spell.* Urbana, IL: National Council for Teachers of English.

Hoffman, P. R., and Norris, J. A. 1989. On the nature of phonological development: Evidence from normal children's spelling errors. *Journal of Speech and Hearing Research* 32:787–94.

Hooper, S. R., Montgomery, J., Swartz, C., Reed, M. S., Sandler, A. D., Levine, M. D., Watson, T. E., and Wasileski, T. 1994. Measurement of written language expression. In *Frames of Reference for the Assessment of Learning Disabilities: New Views of Measurement Issues*, ed. G.R. Lyon. Baltimore: Paul Brookes.

Horn, E. 1969. Spelling. In *Encyclopedia of Educational Research*, 4th ed., ed. R. L. Ebel. New York: Macmillan.

Howard, M. 1982. Utilizing oral-motor feedback in auditory conceptualization. *Journal of Educational Neuropsychology* 2:24–35.

Hull, M. 1985. *Phonics for the Teacher of Reading.* Columbus, OH: Charles Merrill.

Hulme, C., Monk, A., and Ives, S. 1987. Some experimental studies of multisensory teaching: The effects of manual tracing on children's paired-associate learning. *British Journal of Developmental Psychology* 5:299–307.

Invernizzi, M., Abouzeid, M., and Gill, J. T. 1994. Using students' invented spellings as a guide for spelling instruction that emphasizes word study. *Elementary School Journal* 95:155–67.

Invernizzi, M., and M. J. Worthy. 1989. An orthographic-specific comparison of the spelling errors of learning disabled and normal children across four grade levels of spelling achievement. *Reading Psychology: An International Quarterly* 10:173–88.

Jastak, S., and Wilkinson, G. S. 1984. *Wide Range Achievement Test.* Wilmington, DE: Jastak Associates.

Johnson, D. 1986. Remediation for dyslexic adults. In *Dyslexia: Its Neuropsychology and Treatment*, eds. G.T. Pavlidis and D.F. Fisher. Chichester, England: J. Wiley and Sons.

Johnson, D., and Myklebust, H. R. 1967. *Learning Disabilities: Educational Principles and Practices*. New York: Grune and Stratton.

Johnson, K., and Bayrd, P. 1983. *Megawords*. Cambridge, MA: Educators Publishing Service.

Kaufman, A., and Kaufman, N. 1985. *Kaufman Test of Educational Achievement*. Circle Pines, MN: American Guidance Service.

Kent, R. D. 1992. The biology of phonological development. In *Phonological Development: Models, Research, Implications*, eds. C. A. Ferguson, L. Menn, and C. Stoel-Gammon. Timonium, MD: York Press.

Kibel, M., and Miles, T. R. 1994. Phonological errors in the spelling of taught dyslexic children. In *Reading Development and Dyslexia*, eds. C. Hulme and M. Snowling. San Diego, CA: Singular Publishing Group.

King, D. 1984. *Teaching Written Expression to Adolescents*. Cambridge, MA: Educators Publishing Service.

Ladefoged, P. 1982. *A Course in Phonetics*, 2nd ed. San Diego: Harcourt Brace Javanovich.

Larsen, S. C., and Hammill, D. D. 1986. *Test of Written Spelling*. Austin, TX: PRO-ED.

Lecours, A. R. 1966. Serial order in writing: A study of misspelled words in "developmental dysgraphia." *Neuropsychologia* 4:221–4.

Liberman, I. Y., Rubin, H., Duques, S., and Carlisle, J. 1985. Linguistic abilities and spelling proficiency in kindergartners and adult poor spellers. In *Biobehavioral Measures of Dyslexia*, eds. D. B. Gray and J. F. Kavanaugh. Parkton, MD: York Press.

Liberman, I. Y., and Shankweiler. D. 1985. Phonology and the problems of learning to read and write. *Remedial and Special Education* 6:8–17.

Liberman, I. Y., Shankweiler. D., and Liberman, A. M. 1989. The alphabetic principle and learning to read. In *Phonology and Reading Disability: Solving the Reading Puzzle*, eds. D. Shankweiler and I.Y. Liberman. Ann Arbor: University of Michigan Press.

Lindamood, P. 1994. Issues in researching the link between phonological awareness, learning disabilities, and spelling. In *Frames of Reference for the Assessment of Learning Disabilities: New Views on Measurement Issues*, ed. G.R. Lyon. Baltimore, MD: Paul H. Brookes.

Lindamood, C., and Lindamood, P. 1975. *The A.D.D. Program: Auditory Discrimination in Depth* 2nd ed. Columbus, OH: SRA Division, Macmillan/McGraw-Hill.

Lindamood, C., and Lindamood, P. 1979. *Lindamood Auditory Conceptualization Test* 2nd ed. Chicago: Riverside Publishing.

Lindamood, P. C., Bell, N., and Lindamood, P. 1992. Issues in phonological awareness assessment. *Annals of Dyslexia* 42:242–59.

Lovett, M. 1987. A developmental approach to reading disability: Accuracy and speed criteria of normal and deficient reading skills. *Child Development* 58:234–60.

Lundberg, I. 1994. Reading disabilities can be predicted and prevented: A Scandinavian perspective on phonological awareness and reading. In *Reading Development and Dyslexia*, eds. C. Hulme and M. Snowling. San Diego, CA: Singular Publishing Group.

Lyon, G. R., and Moats, L. C. 1988. Critical issues in the instruction of the learning disabled. *Journal of Consulting and Clinical Psychology* 56:830–35.

Mann, V. A. 1993. Phoneme awareness and future reading ability. *Journal of Learning Disabilities* 26:259–69.

Mann, V. A., Tobin, P., and Wilson, R. 1987. Measuring phonological awareness through the invented spellings of kindergarten children. *Merrill Palmer Quarterly* 33:365–91.

Marsh, G., Friedman, M., Welch, V., and Desberg, P. 1981. A cognitive-developmental theory of reading acquisition. In *Reading Research: Advances in Theory and Practice*, eds. G. E. Mackinnon and T. G. Waller. New York: Academic Press.

Meyerson, R. F. 1978. Children's knowledge of selected aspects of sound sattern of English. In *Recent Advances in Psychology of Language: Formal and Experimental Approaches*, eds. R. Campbell and P. Smith. New York: Plenum.

Miles, T. R., and Miles, E. M. 1991. *Dyslexia: A Hundred Years On*. Buckingham: Open University Press.

Mitchell, J., ed. 1985. *The Ninth Mental Measurement Yearbook*. Lincoln, NB: University of Nebraska Press.

Moats, L. C. 1983. A comparison of the spelling errors of older dyslexics and second-grade normal children. *Annals of Dyslexia* 33:121–39.

Moats, L. C. 1993. Assessment of spelling in learning disablties research. In *Frames of Reference for the Assessment of Learning Disabilities: New Views of Measurement Issues*, ed. G. R. Lyon. Baltimore: Paul Brookes.

Moats, L. C. 1993. Spelling error analysis: Beyond the phonetic/dysphonetic dichotomy. *Annals of Dyslexia* 43:174–85

Moats, L. C. 1994. Principles of spelling instruction. In *Teaching Reading: Language, Letters, and Thought*, ed. S. Brody. Milford, NH: LARC Publishing.

Moats, L. C. In press. Phonological spelling errors in the writing of dyslexic adolescents. *Reading and Writing: An Interdisciplinary Journal 8*.

Moats, L. C., and Lyon, G. R. 1993. Learning disabilities in the United States: Science, advocacy and the future of the field. *Journal of Learning Disabilities* 26:282–94.

Moats, L. C., and Smith, C. 1992. Derivational morphology: Why it should be included in assessment and instruction. *Language, Speech and Hearing in the Schools* 23:312–19.

Morris, D. 1982. Word sort: A categorization strategy for improving word recognition ability. *Reading Psychology* 3:247–59.

Morris, D., Blanton, L., Blanton, W. E., Nowacek, J., and Perney, J. (in press). Teaching low achieving students at their instructional level. *Elementary School Journal*.

Morris, D., Nelson, L. J., and Perney, J. 1986. Exploring the concept of "spelling instructional level" through the analysis of error-types. *Elementary School Journal* 87:181–200.

Muschla, G. R. 1991. *The Writing Teacher's Book of Lists*. Englewood Cliffs, NJ: Prentice Hall.

Nelson, H. E. 1980. Analysis of spelling errors in normal and dyslexic children. In *Cognitive Processes in Spelling*, ed. U. Frith. London: Academic Press.

Nulman, J. H., and Gerber, M. M. 1984. Improving spelling performance by imitating a child's errors. *Journal of Learning Disabilities*, 17:328–33.

Olson, R. K. 1985. Disabled reading processes and cognitive profiles. In *Biobehavioral Measures of Dyslexia*, eds. D. Gray and J. Kavanagh. Parkton, MD: York Press.

Parker, F. 1986. *Linguistics for Non-Linguists*. Boston: College-Hill.

Paul, R. 1976. Invented spelling in kindergarten. *Young Children*, 21: 195–200.

Pennington, B. F., McCabe, L. L., Smith, S. D., Lefly, D. L., Bookman, M. O., Kimberling, W. J., and Lubs, H. A. 1986. Spelling errors in adults with a form of familial dyslexia. *Child Development* 57:1001–13.

Posteraro, L., Zinelli, P., and Mazzucchi, A. 1988. Selective impairment of the graphemic buffer in acquired dyslexia: A case study. *Brain and Language* 35:274–86.

Rack, J. P., Snowling, M., and Olson, R. K. 1992. The non-word reading deficit in dyslexia: A review. *Reading Research Quarterly*, 27:28–53.

Read, C. 1971. Preschool children's knowledge of English phonology. *Harvard Educational Review* 41:1–34.

Read, C. 1986. *Children's Creative Spelling*. London: Routledge and Kegan Paul.

Read, C., and Ruyter, L. 1985. Reading and spelling skills in adults of low literacy. *Remedial and Special Education* 6:43–52.

Reith, H., Axelrod, S., Anderson, R., Hathaway, F., Wood, K., and Fitzgerald, C. 1974. Influence of distributed practice and daily testing on weekly spelling tests. *Journal of Educational Research*, 68:73–77.

Richardson, E., and DiBenedetto, B. 1985. *Decoding Skills Test*. Parkton, MD: York Press.

Rohl, E. M., and Tunmer, W. 1988. Phonemic segmentation skill and spelling acquisition. *Applied Psycholinguistics* 9:335–50.

Rosner, J. 1973. *The Perceptual Skills Curriculum*. New York: Walker Educational Book Co.

Rosner, J., and Simon, D. 1971. The Auditory Analysis Test: A preliminary report. *Journal of Learning Disabilities* 4:384–92.

Rubin, H. 1988. Morphological knowledge and early writing ability. *Language and Speech* 31:337:55.

Rubin, H., and Eberhardt, N. C. In press. Facilitating invented spelling through language analysis: An integrated model. *Reading and Writing: An Interdisciplinary Journal* 8.

Rubin, H., Patterson, P. A., and Kantor, P. A. 1991. Morphological development and writing ability in children and adults. *Language, Speech and Hearing Services in the Schools* 22:228–35.

Schlagal, R. C. 1982. A qualitative inventory of word knowledge: A developmental study of spelling, grades one through six. Unpublished doctoral dissertation, University of Virginia, Charlottesville.

Schlagal, R .C. 1986. Informal and qualitative assessment of spelling. *The Pointer* 30:37–41.

Schlagal, R. C. 1992. Patterns of orthographic development in the middle grades. In *Development of Orthographic Knowledge and the Foundations of Literacy*, eds. S. Templeton and D. Bear. Hillsdale, NJ: Lawrence Erlbaum.

Schlagal, R. C., and Schlagal, J. 1992. The integrated character of spelling: Teaching strategies for multiple purposes. *Language Arts* 69:418–24.

Schwartz, S., and Doehring, D. G. 1977. A developmental study of children's ability to acquire knowledge of spelling patterns. *Developmental Psychology* 13: 419–20.

Seidenberg, M., and McClelland, J. 1989. A distributed, developmental model of word recognition and naming. *Psychological Review* 96:523–68.

Seymour, P. 1994. Variability in dyslexia. In *Reading Development and Dyslexia*, ed. C. Hulme and M. Snowling. San Diego, CA: Singular Publishing Group.

Shallice, T. 1981. Phonological agraphia and the lexical route in writing. *Brain* 104:413–29.

Simon, D. P. 1976. Spelling: A task analysis. *Instructional Science* 5:277–302.

Simon, D. P., and Simon, H. A. 1973. Alternative uses of phonemic information in spelling. *Review of Educational Research* 43:115–37.

Snowling, M. 1981 Phonemic deficits in developmental dyslexia. *Psychological Research* 43:219–34.

Snowling, M., and Hulme, C. 1991. Speech processing and learning to spell. In *Language and the Creation of Literacy*, eds. W. Ellis and R. Bowler. Baltimore, MD: The Orton Dyslexia Society.

Snowling, M., Stackhouse, J., and Rack, J. 1986 Phonological dyslexia and dysgraphia —a developmental analysis. *Cognitive Neuropsychology* 3:309–39.

Stanback, M. 1980. Teaching spelling to learning disabled children: Traditional and remedial approaches to spelling instruction. In *Research Review Series, Volume 3*, ed. E. Neuman. New York: Teachers College, Columbia University: Research Institute for the Study of Learning Disabilities.

Stanovich, K. 1988. Explaining the differences between the dyslexic and the garden-variety poor reader: The phonological-core variable-difference model. *Journal of Learning Disabilities* 21:590–604.

Stanovich, K. 1992. Speculations on the causes and consequences of individual differences in early reading acquisition. In *Reading Acquisition*, eds. P. Gough, L. Ehri, and R. Treiman. Hillsdale, NJ: Lawrence Erlbaum.

Steere, A., Peck, C. Z., and Kahn, L. 1971. *Solving Language Difficulties*. Cambridge, MA: Educators Publishing Service.

Sterling, C. M. 1983. Spelling errors in context. *British Journal of Psychology* 74:353–64.

Stoner, J. 1985. *Syllable Plus*. Cambridge, MA: Educators Publishing Service.

Stuart, M., and Coltheart, M. 1988. Does reading develop in a sequence of stages? *Cognition* 30:139–181.

Stuart, M., and Masterson, J. 1992. Patterns of reading and spelling in 10-year old children related to prereading phonological abilities. *Journal of Experimental Child Psychology* 54:168–87.

Sulzby, E. 1980. Word concept development activities. In *Developmental and Cognitive Aspects of Learning to Spell*, eds. E. H. Henderson and J. W. Beers. Newark, DE: International Reading Association.

Sweeney, J. E., and Rourke, B. P. 1985. Spelling disability subtypes. In *Neuropsychology of Learning Disabilities: Essentials of Subtype Analysis*, ed. B. P. Rourke. New York: Guilford Press.

Tangel, D. M., and Blachman, B. A. 1992. Effect of phoneme awareness instruction on kindergarten children's invented spelling. *Journal of Reading Behavior* 24:233–61.

Tangel, D. M., and Blachman, B. A. 1995. Effect of phoneme awareness instruction on the invented spelling of first grade children: A one year follow-up. *Journal of Reading Behavior* 27:153–85.

Templeton, S. 1992. Theory, nature, and pedagogy of higher-order orthographic development in older students. In *Development of Orthographic Knowledge and the Foundations of Literacy*, eds. S. Templeton and D. Bear. Hillsdale, NJ: Lawrence Erlbaum.

Templeton, S., and Bear, D. R., eds. 1992. *Development of Orthographic Knowledge and the Foundations of Literacy: A Memorial Festschrift for Edmund H. Henderson*. Hillsdale, NJ: Lawrence Erlbaum.

Templeton, S., and Scarborough-Franks, L. 1985. The spelling's the thing: Knowledge of derivational morphology in orthography and phonology among older students. *Applied Psycholinguistics* 6:371–90.

Thomson, M. 1991. The teaching of spelling using techniques of simultaneous oral spelling and visual inspection. In *Dyslexia: Integrating Theory and Practice*, eds. M. Snowling and M. Thomson. London: Whurr Publishers.

Torgesen, J., and Bryant, B. 1994. *Test of Phonological Awareness*. Austin, TX: PRO-ED.

Torgesen, J., and Morgan, S. 1992. The effects of two types of phonological awareness training on word learning in kindergarten children. *Journal of Experimental Psychology* 84:364–70.

Treiman, R. 1984. Individual differences among children in spelling and reading styles. *Journal of Experimental Child Pyschology* 37:463–77.

Treiman, R. 1986. The division between onsets and rimes in English syllables. *Journal of Memory and Language* 25:476–91.

Treiman, R. 1993. *Beginning to Spell: A Study of First Grade Children*. New York: Oxford.

Treiman, R., and Baron, J. 1983. Phonemic analysis training helps children benefit from spelling-sound rules. *Memory and Cognition* 11:382–89.

Tunmer, W. E., and Hoover, W. A. 1993. Phonological recoding skill and beginning reading. *Reading and Writing: An Interdisciplinary Journal.* 5:161–79.

Tyler, A., and Nagy, W. 1987. The acquisition of English derivational morphology. (Technical Report No. 407.) Urbana, IL: Center for the Study of Reading.

Uhry, J. K., and Shepherd, M. J. 1993. Segmentation/spelling instruction as part of a first-grade reading program: Effects on several measures of reading. *Reading Research Quarterly* 28:219–33.

Van Orden, G. C., Pennington, B. F., and Stone, G. O. 1990. Word identification in reading and the promise of subsymbolic psycholinguistics. *Psychological Review* 97:488–522.

Vaughn, S. V., Schumm, J. S., and Gordon, J. 1993. Which motoric condition is most effective for teaching spelling to students with and without learning disabilities? *Journal of Learning Disabilities* 26:191–98.

Vellutino, F. 1979. *Dyslexia: Theory and Research*. Cambridge: MIT Press.

Vellutino, F. R., Scanlon, D. M., and Tanzman, M. S. 1994. Components of reading ability: Issues and problems in operationalizing word identification, phonological coding, and orthographic coding. In *Frames of Reference for the Assessment of Learning Disabilities: New Views of Measurement Issues*, ed. G. R. Lyon. Baltimore: Paul Brookes.

Venezky, R. 1967. English orthography: Its graphical structure and its relation to sound. *Reading Research Quarterly* 2:75–105.

Venezky, R. 1970. *The Structure of English Orthography*. The Hague: Mouton.

Viise, N. M. 1992. A comparison of child and adult spelling development. Doctoral Dissertation, University of Virginia, Curry School of Education.

Watson, C., and Willows, D. M. 1993. Evidence for a visual-processing-deficit subtype among disabled readers. In *Visual Processes in Reading and Reading Disabilities*, eds. D. M. Willows, R. S. Kruk, and E. Corcos. Hillsdale, NJ: Lawrence Erlbaum.

Wechsler, D. 1991. *Wechsler Intelligence Scale for Children—3rd Edition*. San Antonio, TX: Psychological Corporation.

Wechsler, D. 1991. *Wechsler Individual Achievement Test*. San Antonio, TX: Psychological Corporation.

White, O. R., and Haring, N. 1980. *Exceptional Teaching* (2nd ed.). Columbus, OH: Charles Merrill.

Wolf, M. 1986. Rapid alternating stimulus naming in the developmental dyslexias. *Brain and Language* 27:360–79.

Woodcock, R. W. 1987. *Woodcock Reading Mastery Test—Revised*. Circle Pines, MN: American Guidance Service.

Woodcock, R. W., and Johnson, M. B. 1989. *Woodcock-Johnson Tests of Achievement—Revised*. Allen, TX: DLM/Teaching Resources.

Worthy, M. J., and Invernizzi, M. 1990. Spelling errors of normal and disabled students on achievement levels one through four: Instructional implications. *Annals of Dyslexia* 40:138–51.

Wysocki, K., and Jenkins, J. R. 1987. Deriving word meanings through morphological generalization. *Reading Research Quarterly* 22:66–81.

Zutell, J. 1992. An integrated view of word knowledge: Correlational studies of the relationships among spelling, reading, and conceptual development. In *Development of Orthographic Knowledge and the Foundations of Literacy: A Memorial Festschrift for Edmund Henderson*, eds. S. Templeton and D. Bear. Hillsdale, NJ: Lawrence Erlbaum.

GLOSSARY

Affix A bound morpheme (meaningful word part) attached to the beginning or end of a base or root that modifies its meaning and creates a derivative. The term includes prefixes, suffixes, and infixes.

Affricate A consonant that consists of a stop followed by a fricative, including the speech sounds that begin the words *chip* and *gypsy*.

Allophone A phonetic variant of a phoneme, such as the /d/ in *dress* and the /d/ in *ladder*.

Alphabetic principle The systematic use of alphabet letters to represent speech sounds or phonemes in a language.

Alveolar ridge The bony ridge right behind the upper front teeth, where the tongue rests to articulate /d/, /t/, and /n/.

Articulation The position of the mouth, tongue, lips, and teeth in the vocal production of speech.

Aspiration The push of air that accompanies the pronunciation of some consonants.

Back vowel A vowel that is articulated with the tongue raised toward the back of the throat; the lips are rounded with most English back vowels.

Bilabial sound A consonant articulated with both lips together, including /b/, /p/, and /m/.

Coarticulation The phenomenon in word pronunciation by which adjacent sounds are often spoken in such a way that one phoneme overlaps, is changed by, and/or modifies another.

Connectionism A theoretical orientation in cognitive psychology that describes the connection weights or strengths of phoneme-grapheme associations and associations among other language units in verbal memory.

Consonant One of a class of speech sounds in which sound moving through the vocal tract is constricted or obstructed during articulation.

Derivation The process of building a new word from another word by adding affixes. For example, the word *destruction* is a derivative of *destruct*, which in turn is derived from *struct*.

Digraph Two adjacent letters that represent one unique phoneme not represented by either letter alone, such as *sh, th, ch, wh,* and *ng*.

Diphthong   A vowel that has two distinct parts with a slide or shift in the middle, as in *boy, bow.*

Distinctive Feature   A feature that distinquishes one phoneme from another.

Dual route theory   A theory of reading and spelling disability that emphasizes the separation of phonological and orthographic processing systems.

Dysgraphia   A poorly defined word referring generally or specifically to a writing problem presumed to be of constitutional origin. It is very common in cases of dyslexia.

Flap   The reduction of /t/ and /d/ in the words *latter* and *ladder* formed by the tongue tapping the alveolar ridge.

Fricative   A consonant produced by partially obstructing the air flow that creates friction and a slight hissing noise, as in /s/ and /f/.

Front vowel   A vowel articulated with the tongue raised toward the front of the mouth.

Glide   A vowel-like consonant, /w/ and /y/.

Grapheme   A letter or group of letters that represents one speech sound. Most graphemes are more than one letter.

Homophone   A word that sounds like another but has a different spelling and a different meaning, such as *bear* and *bare.*

Inflection   An affix that creates or shows the tense, number, or person of a verb, the plural or possessive forms, or the comparative forms.

Lax vowel   Otherwise called a "short" vowel in phonics.

Lexical   Of or relating to words or the vocabulary of the language; or the meaning of the base word in inflected and derived forms.

Linguistic awareness   Implicit or explicit awareness of language structure and form that allows the conscious manipulation of language and reflection on language.

Liquid   A class of sounds that contains /l/ and /r/.

Morpheme   The smallest meaningful linguistic unit.

Morphology   The internal structure of words and the relationships among words in a language; also the study of word formation patterns.

Nasalized vowel   A vowel in which air is pushed through the nose; all vowels before nasal consonants in English are nasalized.

Obstruent   A class of consonants that includes stops, fricatives, and affricates.

Onset   The initial consonant(s) of a syllable, before the vowel.

Orthography   The writing system of a language.

Palatal   The place of articulation involving the tongue against the bony structure at the roof of the mouth; /y/ is a palatal consonant.

Phoneme   The smallest unit of speech that makes a difference to meaning.

Phonetics   The study of the way in which speech sounds are articulated; also the systematic classification of the inventory of speech sounds in a language.

Phonics   The system by which symbols represent sounds in an alphabetic orthography.

Phonological rules   Unconscious rules governing speech sound production and the sequence in which sounds can be produced.

Rime   The last part of a syllable, including the vowel and what follows it.

Semantics   The study of word meanings.

Sonorant   Nasal, liquid, and glide consonants as a class of phonemes that are not obstruents.

Stop Consonant   A consonant that is produced with a complete obstruction of air.

Syllable   A spoken unit that must have a vowel and that includes the consonants that precede or follow that vowel.

Syntax   The rule system by which words may be ordered in phrases and sentences.

Tense vowel   Otherwise known as "long" vowels in English phonics.

Velar articulation   Pronunciation of sounds with the tongue against the back roof of the mouth, including /k/ and /g/.

Voiced consonant   A consonant articulated with vocal vibration.

Voiceless (unvoiced) consonant   A consonant articulated with no vocal vibration.

Vowel   A class of open speech sounds that are not consonants.

APPENDIX A

160 Common Words Grouped by Spelling Patterns

Although many of these high frequency words often appear on "irregular" word lists or are taught as "sight" words, many can often be grouped with other words by their sound-spelling patterns.

Loners, no family: a, the, I, of, was, are, they, what, were, said, who, very, people, water, know, use, received, these

Short vowel regular words:

am	is, his	not, got, box
an, and, man, can, ran, than	it	
as, has	in, into	
at, cat	if	
had, glad	him	
back, black	did, big	
	with, this, which, think	
run, fun	when, then, them	put
us, just, bus, but	get, let	look, book, good
up, much	red, send	would, could, should
	yes	

Long vowel pattern words:

each	he	so	way	make	time	to	seen	by
please	we	go	day	made	like	do	see	my
dear	she	no	may	came	write		(been)	
	me		say	ride			green	
	be		play	home				

R-controlled vowel famlies:

over	there	here	word	for	part	her	girl
order	letter	(heir)	work	or	car		first
letter				more	far		
number				before			
after							
other							

Diphthongs and other vowel families:

oil	how	about	from
boy, toy	now	out	some
	brown		come
	cow		done
	down		one
			once

Other patterns:

two	many	you	have
twice	any	your	love
twenty		yours	give
twelve		our	
will	old	ball	
well	told	call	
	cold	all	

APPENDIX B

Examples of Spelling Alternatives for Selected Speech Sounds

Examples of Spelling Alternatives for Selected Speech Sounds

Consonants

/f/	fan	puff	sphere	phantom	tough
	deaf	skiff	sphynx	siphon	laugh
	flirt	off	sphincter	graph	rough
	swift	staff			

/g/	get	ghoul	vague		
	big	ghost	intrigue		
	gander	ghastly	analogue		

/j/	jam	gem	edge	village	educate
	jiffy	gym	dodge	slippage	individual
	job	gist	fudge	carnage	arduous

/k/	kite	cat	sock	chorus	baroque
	kitchen	comb	duck	chaos	antique
	kettle	cusp	wreck	orchestra	boutique

/m/	merry	bomb	mnemonic		
	member	climb	hymn		
	promenade	succumb	autumn		

/n/	nap	knack	gnat	pneumonia	
	bind	know	gnaw	pneumatics	
	penny	knee	gnostic		

/ŋ/	sing	sink	language		
	bang	bank	English		
	wrong	honky-tonk	finger		

127

/r/	rest	burr	wreck	rheumatic	
	very	whirr	wrap	rhythm	
	parch	shirr	wrist	rhyme	

/s/	saint	cyst	pass	scissors	psychology
	sorry	cinch	mess	ascend	psalm
	suction	cease	fuss	scenic	pseudo

/t/	tough	butt	doubt	walked	
	terry	watt	debt	pepped	
	tumble	boycott		psyched	

/z/	zoo	dogs	xerox	
	zesty	result	xylo	
	zig-zag	dads	xenophobe	

/š/	ship	sugar	partial	mission	facial	chagrin
	stash	sure	station	session	special	chef
	sheer		patience	passion	conscience	charlatan

/č/	chop	ditch	future	mention	
	poach	wretch	picture	tension	
	screech	catcher	denture	unctuous	

/zh/	treasure	vision	
	azure	persuasion	

/kw/	quack	awkward	
	acquiesce	bookworm	
	question		

/ks/	box	sinks	panics	socks
	axe	peeks	picnics	racks
	except	beatniks		

/gz/	exit	
	exact	
	exhume	

/sk/	skin	scream	schism	squeamish
	ask	scary	school	square
	desk	scald	schooner	squash

/kr/	cry	chrome	
	cramp	Christmas	
	acrid	chronic	

Vowels

/e/	baby	safe	rain	play		
	radio	fame	waist	fray		
	vein	they	sleigh	steak		
	skein	hey	eight	great		
/i/	secret	these	feet	eat		
	recent	cheese	sleep	dear		
	chief	candy	please			
	piece	baby	easy			
/aj/	tiger	pine	night			
	migrate	bite	sigh			
	pie	type	my			
	die	graphyte	cry			
/o/	pony	home	boat	snow	toe	
	bromide	stone	loam	crow	doe	
/ju/	music	mule	few	value	suit	Europe
/u/	lunar	flute	flew	true	nuisance	
	moon	soup				
/ɛ/	head	bed				
	steady	elephant				
	treasure	escalator				
/I/	itchy	gym				
	pinch	cryptic				
/ɔj/	oil	boy				
	poison	employ				
/aw/	ouch	cow				
	mouse	flower				
/ɔ/	saw	Paul	daughter	bought		
	fawn	autumn	aught	thought		
/ər/	her	bird	turn	word		
	nerd	stir	Thursday	worth		

APPENDIX C

Helpful Resources for Teaching Spelling

Cohen, C. R. 1987. *Spellmaster*. Austin, TX: PRO-ED.

Forbes, C. T. 1968. *Graded and Classified Spelling Lists for Teachers, Grades 2-8*. Cambridge, MA: Educators Publishing Service.

Graham, S., Harris, K. R., and Loynachan, C. 1994. The spelling for writing list. *Journal of Learning Disabilities* 27:210-14.

Henderson, E. 1990. *Teaching Spelling* 2nd Ed. Boston: Houghton Miflin.

Henry, M. 1990. *Words*. Los Gatos, CA: Lex Press.

Hodges, R. E. 1982. *Improving Spelling and Vocabulary in the Secondary School*. National Council for Teachers of English, 1111 Kenyon Road, Urbana, Illinois 61801.

Hodges, R. E. 1981. *Learning To Spell*. National Council for Teachers of English, 1111 Kenyon Road, Urbana, Illinois 61801.

Orton, J. L. 1976. *A Guide to Teaching Phonics*. Cambridge, MA: Educators Publishing Service.

Rudginsky, L. T., and Haskell, E. C. 1984. *How to Teach Spelling*. Cambridge, MA: Educators Publishing Service.

Slingerland, B. H. and Murray, C. 1978. *Teachers's Word Lists for Reference, To Accompany a Multi-sensory Approach to Language Arts for Specific Language Disability Children*. Cambridge, MA: Educators Publishing Service.

INDEX